Thomas
Cook

TRAVELLERS

BUDAPEST

By
LOUIS JAMES

Written by Louis James, updated by Wendy Wrangham
Original photography by Ken Patterson

Published by Thomas Cook Publishing
A division of Thomas Cook Tour Operations Limited.
Company registration no. 1450464 England
The Thomas Cook Business Park, 9 Coningsby Road,
Peterborough PE3 8SB, United Kingdom
E-mail: sales@thomascook.com, Tel: + 44 (0) 1733 416477
www.thomascookpublishing.com

Produced by Cambridge Publishing Management Limited
Burr Elm Court, Main Street, Caldecote CB23 7NU

ISBN: 978-1-84157-843-9

© 2003, 2006 Thomas Cook Publishing
This third edition © 2008
Text © Thomas Cook Publishing
Maps © Thomas Cook Publishing

Series Editor: Maisie Fitzpatrick
Production/DTP: Steven Collins

Printed and bound in Italy by Printer Trento

Cover photography: Front L-R: © Pignatelli Massimo/SIME-4Corners Images,
© Paul Panayiotou/4Corners Images; © Giovanni Simeone/SIME-4Corners
Images. Back L-R: © Anna Watson/Getty Images/Axiom RM; © Cozzi
Guido/4Corners Images

FSC

Mixed Sources
Product group from well-managed
forests and recycled wood or fibre

Cert no. CQ-COC-000012
www.fsc.org
© 1996 Forest Stewardship Council

Contents

KEY TO MAPS

Ⓜ Underground

ⓘ Information

★ Start of walk

◆◆◆◆ Funicular railway

Introduction

At the end of the 19th century a traveller to Budapest neatly described the enigmatic quality of the city: 'If one is travelling from the east in the direction of Western Europe, it is in Budapest that one experiences the breath of Western civilisation. However, if one is travelling in the opposite direction, it is here that one first gets a taste of the East . . .'

When the seven Magyar (Hungarian) tribes came over the Carpathians more than 1,000 years ago, one group of them pitched their tents at this strategic point on the mighty River Danube. Although they were always to retain a proud memory of their Asian origins, they now began a new and settled existence in Europe.

In the Middle Ages the Royal Castle of Buda and its ancillary town grew wealthy under Magyar, Anjou (Angevin) and Luxembourg rulers. The subsequent 150-year-long Turkish occupation, and the Habsburg rule that followed, then reduced Buda to provincial status. In the mid-19th century the hitherto insignificant town of Pest rapidly expanded into a great industrial metropolis. Until around 1860, half its inhabitants were German-speaking and there was also a large influx of Jews; most of the latter rapidly assimilated and became leading figures in the arts and in business. By 1900, Buda and Pest (united since 1873) had acquired the patina of mixed culture and unbridled

WHAT IT MEANS TO BE A MAGYAR

'Anyone who wants to understand Hungary,' writes the poet and journalist István Eörsi, 'needs to find the answer to one great secret: how is it that this country has survived at all? . . . No nation is so experienced in defeat as the Hungarians.' This feeling of being the victims of history is recurrent in the Magyar psyche.

On two occasions in the past – when the Tartars invaded in the 13th century and during the Turkish occupation – there was a real danger of national extinction. In the 18th century the German philosopher Johann Herder predicted that the Magyar nation and culture would soon disappear, absorbed by their Slav and German neighbours.

It is language that most isolates Hungarians. Arthur Koestler summed up the fears and contradictions in the Magyars' image of themselves: 'To be Hungarian is a collective neurosis.'

and have-nots has widened rapidly since 1989.

Hotels, apartment buildings and shopping centres are popping up all over the city, but the homeless, the beggars and the hard-pressed pensioners remain.

On the credit side, Hungarians are natural entrepreneurs and much is being done to make the city buzz again. Despite political wobbles and a 10 per cent GDP public sector deficit, the government's austerity programme has won economic plaudits and there are grounds for optimism.

However, don't expect Hungarians to admit that things have improved. As the local saying goes: 'A pessimist is only a well-informed optimist'.

capitalism which has now reappeared after 40 years of suspended animation under Communism.

Back to the future

As in other cities of the former Eastern Bloc, the gap between the haves

Introduction

On the banks of the River Danube

The city

Budapest lies 47 degrees 23 minutes north and 19 degrees 9 minutes east, on either side of the River Danube (Duna). Within the river's 28km (17-mile) passage through the city, the width of the channel varies between 1km (²/₃ mile) and 230m (755ft). The mighty waterway has shaped the character of the city. For the Romans it was a defensive barrier – they built their garrison and administrative capital at Aquincum on the western bank. The Magyar kings shifted the focus to the natural citadel of Buda Hill, while Pest was the gateway to the east, a town of travellers and traders, later the dynamic centre of business and industry.

In the landscape, too, the characteristics of the two cities reflect different aspects of Hungary: from the flattish terrain of Pest, the Alföld (Great Hungarian Plain) stretches to the east and south; on the west bank the gentle hills of Buda (the highest is the 529m/1,735ft János hegy) point the way to the rolling landscapes of Transdanubia.

Economy

The government is tightening its belt after a splurge to win the 2006 election.

THOMAS COOK'S BUDAPEST

In 1885, Cook's were appointed official travel agents for the agricultural exhibition staged by the Hungarian government. The first Thomas Cook office in Budapest was opened three years later. Cook's were active in promoting Hungary's Millennial Exhibition in 1896 and Budapest spas in the 1930s.

Inflation soared to 9 per cent in early 2007, but is projected to settle at around 5 per cent. The staggering budget deficit is expected to drop to 6.4 per cent of GDP and economic growth has slowed to around 2.4 per cent. However, foreign investment and the travel and tourism sector are growing and should help to revitalise the economy.

Environment

Like other former Eastern Bloc cities, Budapest still suffers from decaying infrastructure and serious pollution. With EU status comes stricter environmental policy, and the initiative to get smoke-belching Trabants off the roads has proved successful. Power stations have been made cleaner and more efficient, although a second nuclear station is being touted to limit

Hungary's dependence on Russian gas (80 per cent of consumption annually).

Budapest's water supply remains endangered by the Slovak government's decision to persist with the Gabčíkovo hydroelectric dam on the Danube, a project from which Hungary withdrew in 1992. The International Court of Justice has determined that the treaty is still valid, but Hungary has ignored the ruling. The fertile agricultural area of Szigetköz in western Hungary is badly affected. However, the reduction of fuel emissions and the cleaning of public buildings have given Budapest a new face. Investment in infrastructure will take longer, but the telephone system has been modernised. The M0 ring road motorway has suffered delays and debts and officials hope for completion in the first half of 2008.

GOODBYE TRABI!

An elegiac piece in the press of 1991 lamented the passing of East German imports – the 'Trabi' (Trabant), which provided an experience 'like riding a four-wheel moped in a raincoat'; the Practica 35mm SLR, 'a good workhorse camera designed for planets without gravity'; and 'nifty kitchen wares made of slag-iron'.

Pollution has taken a heavy toll on many of Pest's façades

History

AD 106   The Roman garrison of Aquincum (in Óbuda) becomes the capital of Lower Pannonia.

5th century   According to legend, Attila the Hun ruled from the abandoned Roman amphitheatre in Aquincum. His brother, Bleda, is supposed to have given his name to a new city – 'Buda'.

896   Seven Magyar tribes under Árpád cross the Carpathians and settle on the Danubian plains.

Late 10th century   The Magyar Prince Géza converts to Christianity; his son Vajk is baptised as István (Stephen).

1000   Stephen is crowned King of Hungary on Christmas Day, with a crown sent by the Pope. Between 997 and 1038, King (later Saint) Stephen turns Hungary into a Christian feudal state.

1061   The first documentary reference about Pest.

1241   Tartar (Mongol) invaders virtually destroy Hungary.

To rebuild it, King Béla IV invites Germans and other foreigners to settle. The Castle of Buda is built (1247–65).

1301   The Hungarian Árpád line dies out. The House of Anjou succeeds, followed by Sigismund of Luxembourg in 1387.

1458–90   Under Matthias I (Corvinus), Buda achieves its golden age.

1526–41   Buda falls to the Turks.

1686   Armies led by Charles of Lorraine and Eugene of Savoy reconquer Buda. Hungary falls under Habsburg rule.

1710–11   Buda and Pest are blockaded during the War of Independence waged by Ferenc Rákóczi II.

1795   A Jacobin revolt is crushed. Archduke Joseph (son of Leopold II) becomes Palatine (Viceroy) of Hungary.

1848   Hungary, under Lajos Kossuth, briefly achieves

independence from Habsburg rule.

1867	Franz Joseph and Ferenc Deák negotiate the Ausgleich (Compromise) to create the Austro-Hungarian Empire.
1872–73	The towns of Buda, Óbuda and Pest are united to form Budapest.
1896	The Millennial Celebrations mark 1,000 years of Hungary's existence.
1918–19	The Austro-Hungarian Empire collapses; the Hungarian Republic is proclaimed. The Communist Republic of Councils is formed.
1920	By the Treaty of Trianon, Hungary loses two-thirds of its territory. Three million Hungarians are marooned in the Empire's successor states.
1945–8	Soviet armies 'liberate' Budapest; the Communists seize power.
1956	Soviet armies invade Hungary to suppress a popular anti-Commuist rebellion. János Kádár forms a puppet regime.

1988	Kádár is ousted; an interim government of reform Communists works for free elections.
1990	Right-of-centre Hungarian Democratic Forum led by József Antall wins elections.
1990–94	Sweeping market reforms, but living standards fall.
1994	Socialists and Free Democrats win elections.
1998	The right-of-centre Hungarian Civic Party under Viktor Orbán forms a government with the Smallholders' Party.
2002	Socialists and Free Democrats regain power.
2004	Hungary becomes a member of the EU on 1 May.
2006	In April over 10,000 troops and police battle record flood waters of the Danube. October sees violent anti-government protests during the 50th anniversary commemorations of the 1956 uprising. Protestors demand the resignation of the prime minister after he admits to lying in elections.

1956 and all that

The heroism of the Hungarian revolution of 1956 has passed into history – a brave battle against appalling odds. For a few brief days of euphoria, it looked as if it might succeed, and the Stalinist tyranny seemed on the brink of extinction.

Pressure for change came first from the so-called 'Petőfi Circle', named after Hungary's national poet and freedom fighter. Then student demonstrations attracted thousands of supporters. Finally, factory workers became the driving force of the revolution. Much of the Hungarian army, led by Pál Maléter, also fought for freedom.

TIMETABLE OF A REVOLUTION
6 October 1956
200,000 people attend the reburial of László Rajk, the Interior Minister executed after a show-trial by the Rákosi regime.

Statue of Imre Nagy, silhouetted against the Parliament building

23 October

In solidarity with the Polish opposition, students lead a march to the statue of the Polish general and Hungarian freedom fighter József Bem.

At 6pm, Imre Nagy, previously expelled from the Party for his espousal of a more humane government as prime minister in 1953, speaks to vast crowds before the Parliament.

At 11pm, students besiege the radio station and the ÁVH (Security Service) open fire on them.

24 October

Imre Nagy becomes prime minister. Soviet tanks move on to Budapest.

31 October

A truce is arranged and Soviet tanks withdraw.

1 November

Nagy announces that Hungary is to leave the Warsaw Pact.

3 November

Pál Maléter, negotiating with the Soviet Army under guarantee of safe conduct, is arrested.

4 November

Soviet Army reinvades. János Kádár announces the formation of his puppet government. Nagy flees to the Yugoslav embassy.

22 November

Nagy leaves the Yugoslav embassy with a promise of safe conduct and is arrested.

16 June 1958

Nagy and Maléter are executed.

AFTERMATH OF THE REVOLUTION

While the borders remained open, 200,000 people fled the country. There were an estimated 2,000 revenge executions; thousands more were imprisoned.

16 June 1989

Some 250,000 people attended a ceremony on Heroes' Square to honour Imre Nagy and Pál Maléter, whose remains were reburied.

6 July 1989

On the day the Supreme Court declared Nagy innocent of the charges on which he was convicted and executed, János Kádár died.

'If my life is necessary to prove that not all Communists are enemies of the people, then I willingly give it up.'
IMRE NAGY, reportedly his last words in 1958.

Politics

In 1989 the Soviet Union's satellite regimes buckled one by one under the combined pressure of failing economies and Mikhail Gorbachev's policy of glasnost *(openness). The smooth transition from totalitarianism to democracy was possible in Hungary chiefly because the last Communist government accepted the inevitable gracefully.*

The end of Communism

During János Kádár's long rule (1956–88), the oppressive paraphernalia of Stalinism had been softened and a small private sector allowed to develop. This had led to Hungary being regarded as 'the happiest barracks in the Socialist camp'. But in the 1980s, the country suffered from rising inflation and an alarming increase in foreign debt. The ageing Kádár compounded his economic mismanagement by the decision to go ahead with the construction of an ecologically catastrophic dam at Nagymaros on the Danube, part of a joint energy project with the Slovaks.

At the May 1988 Party Congress, reformers and technocrats joined forces to oust Kádár from the leadership. By July 1989 four of them, under the impressive leadership of the youthful Miklós Németh, were in control of the government. By October the Communists had reconstituted themselves as the Socialist Party, the 'iron curtain' on the Austrian border had been dismantled, and free elections announced for the following year. In November, on the 33rd anniversary of the 1956 revolution (*see pp10–11*), the Republic of Hungary was proclaimed.

The elections of 1990

Two parties dominated the second round of voting (25 March): the populist and conservative Hungarian Democratic Forum and the intellectual metropolitan Alliance of Free Democrats, with the Democratic Forum emerging a clear winner. A worrying sign was the low turnout, which seemed to indicate that much of the electorate expected very little to be achieved by any political grouping. The government subsequently formed by József Antall was a coalition that included the revived Smallholders' Party (winners of the last free elections in 1945, but now a sentimental relic) and the Christian Democrats. A distinguished Free Democrat and former Communist victim, Árpád Göncz, was elected president by Parliament.

The Antall government

In facing the severe economic and political problems inherited from Communism, the Antall government looked increasingly beleaguered. Its image was also tarnished by the right wing of the Democratic Forum, led by the writer István Csurka, indulging in anti-Semitic rhetoric and demanding witch-hunts against former Communists.

Until his death in December 1993, Antall ploughed on with his strategy of gradual adjustment to the free market economy. But while fiscal retrenchment and conscientious debt servicing preserved Hungary's credit rating on the financial markets, inflation at over 20 per cent, high unemployment and social hardship produced a Socialist victory in the 1994 elections.

Hungary at the crossroads

In the 21st century, there are many negative factors in Hungarian life. The economy has been buffeted by the world recession and society has been hamstrung by the contrast between the poverty of many and the wealth of a few. The public frequently turns in disgust from politicians seemingly more interested in the spoils of power than in the enlightened use of it. Yet there are also grounds for optimism. Hungarians are entrepreneurial and resourceful as a nation: if the opportunities arise, they will be quick to seize them.

Growth is continuing and the country has attracted the most foreign investment of the former Eastern Bloc countries. The alliance between prime minister Ferenc Gyurcsány's Socialist Party and the Liberal Party remains, despite massive social unrest in late 2006 after Gyurcsány admitted to lying. Despite this, his coalition easily won a resulting vote of no confidence.

Freedom Monument on Gellért Hegy

People and culture

The numerous warm, healing springs of the Budapest area attracted settlers from earliest times, the first of them occupying the limestone caves formed by spa waters on the Danube's west bank. Eventually these spas (see pp38–9) were to become a significant source of wealth for the inhabitants. The Danube itself was crucial to the development of Hungary, bringing trade and valuable immigrants, as well as less welcome invaders and floods.

The historic name of the Hungarian people is 'Magyars', 'Hungary' being 'Magyarország'. Now much diluted, the Magyars are descended from the Ugrian branch of the Finno-Ugric people who once populated the land between the Urals and the River Ob. While their northern cousins, the Finns and Estonians, are descendants of the group that migrated north and west around 2000 BC, the Magyars were influenced by Turkic and other cultures around the Caucasus before crossing into the Carpathian Basin in AD 896.

City population

Buda and Pest have had a mixed population since early times, including foreign craftsmen and merchants. Large numbers of Germans were settled by the Austrian Empress Maria Theresa in order to rebuild the country after 150 years of Turkish devastation; then in the 19th century thousands of Jews migrated to Hungary from Moravia and Galicia, the majority settling in Pest.

Today, the population of Budapest is nearly two million, one in five of the Hungarians living within Hungary. Some five million live beyond the borders, most of them as minorities in neighbouring countries. Movement out of Budapest to the wider conurbation is increasing.

Religion

Hungary has been Christian since the 11th century, when King Stephen forcibly converted the population. Although Orthodoxy had a toehold of influence through royal marriages, the country was firmly Catholic until the Reformation, but 90 per cent of Hungarians had become Protestant by the late 16th century. Habsburg rule and its attendant Counter-Reformation sought to reverse this situation, but Protestantism hung on in the east and on the Great Plain. Today, Hungary is 57 per cent Catholic and 30 per cent Protestant.

Statue of Franz Liszt by László Martou on the square named after him

A European culture

Hungary's artistic legacy reflects the country's attachment to the traditions of Western European culture, and the further back we look, the more apparent this becomes. From the establishment of the feudal state under King Stephen (997–1038) until the Turkish invasions in the 16th century, Hungary was part of the supranational European Christian culture. Artists and craftsmen came from the Low Countries, Germany and Italy to work for the Hungarian kings of the late Árpád, Anjou and Luxembourg dynasties. The Cistercian, Benedictine and Premonstratensian orders built churches in the pan-European Romanesque and Gothic styles: fine examples have survived at Ják in western Hungary and Bélapátfalva in the east.

The palaces of Buda and Visegrád (*see pp48 & 123*) reached the summit of splendour under King Matthias Corvinus (1458–90), who invited the best Italian craftsmen to work there. His Renaissance court was a glittering centre of the arts and humanist scholarship. Half a century later Hungary was dismembered in the Turkish wars; Transylvania retained its political and cultural autonomy under the leadership of Protestant princes, but the rest of the territory was carved up between the Turks and the Habsburgs.

The rise of national culture

The expulsion of the Turks at the end of the 17th century brought with it the Counter-Reformation and Habsburg dominance. The baroque town of Buda and baroque churches in Pest date from this period. National resistance to the Austrian oppressors was conducted through warfare in the 18th century, but increasingly found expression through culture after Emperor Joseph II (1780–90) tried to Germanise his Hungarian subjects. The epics of Mihály Vörösmarty (1800–55) revived consciousness of Magyar history and the poet Sándor Petőfi became a hero of the 1848 war of independence against the Habsburgs. The early 19th-century architecture of Pest, while reflecting the Central European taste for neoclassicism, was created by Hungarian masters such as Mihály Pollack and József Hild. Later in the 19th century, Miklós Ybl built many of the great neo-Renaissance palaces on the graceful boulevards of the expanding city.

Back to the roots

In the late 19th century, we encounter a different kind of Hungarian self-perception, one that reconciles semi-mythical Eastern roots with Western civilisation. The national revival in literature began with the proclamation by Ferenc Kölcsey (author of the Hungarian national anthem) that poetry must be sought 'in the songs of the common people', while in the late 19th century architects and artists began to cultivate a consciously

Hungarian manner. Ödön Lechner (*see pp66–7*) was one such architect, and Károly Kós (*see p137*), in the early years of the 20th century, drew inspiration from Transylvanian vernacular forms and the English Arts and Crafts Movement. The latter also influenced the members of the Gödöllő artists' colony, founded in 1902 near Budapest, whose work exploited Hungarian folk motifs. In the fine arts the *plein-air* school of Nagybánya produced distinctively Hungarian landscape paintings, while the idiosyncratic work of Tivadar Csontváry Kosztka embodied a mystical sense of Hungarian identity.

In music, Franz Liszt was the first to popularise Hungarian themes. He also founded the Budapest Music Academy, which was to nurture innumerable great talents. In 1905 Béla Bartók and Zoltán Kodály began their great work of systematically collecting Hungarian folk music from all over the country and this was to influence their own music.

People and culture

The Royal Palace of Buda

Impressions

The outskirts of Budapest are little different from those of other cities of the former Eastern Bloc: decaying factories ring the Pest side and blocks of prefabricated 'panel housing' disfigure the skyline. Luckily, Budapest is still a modest-sized city by contemporary European standards and the centre is quickly reached from the airport.

The historic cores of Pest and Buda hug opposite banks of the Danube. You can gain an overall impression of them by taking one of the trams that run along either side of the river (from Jászai Mari tér or Batthyány tér); or you could climb to the Halászbástya (Fishermen's Bastion) on Castle Hill for a bird's-eye view of Pest.

Pest is a bustling, lively town with towering 19th-century blocks and great boulevards. At first it is easy to get lost in the urban density of the Belváros (Inner City); but a few minutes' walk in any direction brings you to a major landmark, square or avenue. By contrast, residential Buda is on a smaller scale and more private, while Castle Hill is an historical tableau.

In his *Budapest Walks* in 1916, city chronicler Gyula Krúdy wrote: 'This city smells of violets in the spring, as do the ladies along the promenade above the river on the Pest side. In the autumn, it is Buda that suggests the tone: the odd thud of chestnuts dropping on the castle walk, fragments of the music of a military band wafting over the forlorn silence: autumn and Buda were born of the same mother.' Today, though a Transylvanian fiddler may have replaced the military band and ladies on the promenade are redolent of high fashion names like Louis Vuitton or Hilfiger rather than the scent of violets, nostalgia is in: Budapest is selling old style to a new clientele.

When to go

Central Europe's continental climate is extremely hot in summer, raw and cold in winter. The nicest times to visit are between April and the end of June and, especially, between September and the end of October. The long Indian summer provides ideal weather for excursions (*see p120*). If you must visit in high summer, you can keep cool by heading for the spas (*see pp38–9*) during the heat of the day and lodging in the Buda Hills rather than down in the stifling city. August sees the spectacular fireworks display above the Danube which usually marks the beginning of the end of the *canicula* – as Hungarians call the broiling midsummer season.

The Budapest Arts Weeks kick off on the anniversary of Béla Bartók's birth (25 September). Annual events include a wine festival, an international dog show in May, and the Budapest Spring Festival in the second half of March.

Arriving

Direct flights from European capitals and America arrive at Ferihegy, Budapest's international airport, 24km (15 miles) to the east of the city centre. Budapest has several daily rail connections to Vienna and Prague, all trains now arriving at and leaving from the Keleti pályaudvar (Eastern Railway Station). Keleti pályaudvar has a metro connection to the city centre and is also served by numerous bus, trolleybus and tram routes. Now almost all international trains use Keleti pályaudvar, while Nyugati pályaudvar (Western Railway Station) and Déli pályaudvar (Southern Railway Station) serve domestic destinations. From April to October a hydrofoil runs once daily on the Danube between Vienna and Budapest, taking five and a half hours.

The majority of travellers by car arrive via Vienna, which is well served by the German/Austrian Autobahn network. A new motorway now runs from Vienna to Budapest, the Hungarian section being a toll road. You must buy a vignette (sticker) to use it (*www.autopalya.hu*). An Autobahn sticker must be purchased for the

Buda, Pest and the Danube

Impressions

Austrian section and (after crossing the border) also for the Hungarian section (available at petrol stations and special sales points after crossing the border). Make sure that your registration number is carefully recorded on it.

Getting around

Getting around in Budapest is no great problem for the visitor, although unpronounceable names may cause difficulties at first. The areas of interest to visitors are relatively small and compact, and are well served by metro, trams, trolleybuses and buses. It is advisable to buy an up-to-date street plan on arrival – some street names were still being changed even in the 1990s. It is worth buying the modestly priced three-day tourist ticket (*túristajegy 3 napra*) or seven-day ticket (*hetijegy*) valid on all forms of city transport and on sale at larger metro stations. The Budapest Card, valid for 48 or 72 hours, includes not only public transport, but also free admission to 60 museums and other sights, as well as eligibility for discounts at various places.

The metro has three lines, colour coded and numbered: M1 = yellow, M2 = red, M3 = blue. All meet at the central junction on Deák Ferenc tér. The blue line runs across Pest, the red one crosses the Danube to south Buda, and the yellow follows the radial Andrássy útca through the centre of Pest. Red trolleybuses run only on the Pest side. Yellow trams run along either side of the Danube, along the Pest

Chain Bridge (Széchenyi lánchíd)

boulevards and on main arteries elsewhere. There is also an excellent bus service (buses are blue). Be aware that you need to press the button near the door if you wish to get off, and also the button outside the door, in newer buses, trams and trolleybuses, if the door has not opened and you wish to board the vehicle. The HÉV suburban railway (green trains) is useful for excursions (to Szentendre from Batthyány tér, Ráckeve from Kőzvágóhíd or Gödöllő from Örs vezér tere, although rides to this neighbouring city need a supplementary ticket, *see pp128, 130–1 & 136*). More transport details are given in the **Practical Guide** on p186.

Other means of transport in Budapest are principally for sightseeing. The boats criss-crossing the Danube afford views of the Országház (Parliament) and Buda Castle from the river; a cable car (Sikló) runs up to Castle Hill from Clark Ádám tér; a chairlift takes you from Zugliget to János-hegy in the Buda Hills; a cogwheel railway (Fogaskerekű) runs from Városmajor on the Buda side up to Széchenyi hegy (Széchenyi Hill); the Children's Railway (*see p152*) runs through the Buda woods.

Taxis are cheap by Western standards. There are rather too many rogues – stick to the well-established companies: Budataxi, City Taxi and Főtaxi (which has the best reputation).

Manners and mores

Hungarians do not expect foreigners to master their language, but it is best to learn greetings, which are always offered on entering or leaving a shop or in addressing strangers. These are: *jó reggelt* (good morning), *jó napot* (good day – from about 10am), *jó estét* (good evening) and *jó éjszakát* (goodnight). *Viszontlátásra* is goodbye (*see* Language in the **Practical Guide** on *p185*). Silence or a nod could be taken as rudeness.

When you introduce yourself or are introduced, always shake hands and say your complete name. Your interlocutor will do likewise, but remember that Hungarian names are in reverse order, whether written or spoken. Thus, Englishman John Smith meets Hungarian Kovács János (Smith John).

Hungarians are extremely hospitable, and proud housewives will probably press on you more food than you want. Trying to foot the bill in a restaurant is usually a struggle – accept *force majeure* with good grace unless there are compelling reasons for not doing so. If you are invited to somebody's home, flowers for the hostess and perhaps wine for the host are usual. You may be asked to remove your shoes and put on house slippers – simply to protect the invariably spotless home! When it comes to the meal, never drink before your host has raised his glass and wished everyone good health.

Feminists will note that male chauvinism is alive and well, often masquerading as old-style gallantry. Yet battle-hardened ladies have been known to melt just a little when greeted with *kezét csókolom* (I kiss your hand).

Fiakers can be used for painless sightseeing on Castle Hill

Budapest

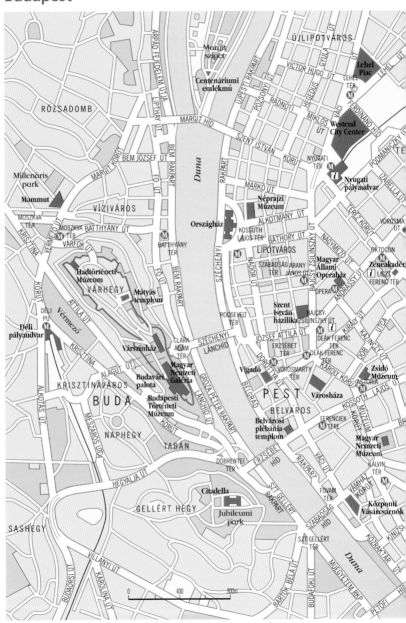

AREAS OF BUDAPEST
Administration

For administrative purposes Budapest is divided into 23 districts, of which about 10 will be of interest to the visitor. The others are primarily residential or industrial. District numbers are required for postcodes, but otherwise people stick to names sanctioned by custom and use.

Districts of Buda

The Buda side of the Danube is dominated by Várhegy (Castle Hill), below which is Víziváros (Water Town) stretching as far as Moszkva tér behind the hill's northern tip.

To the northwest is Rózsadomb (the Hill of Roses), where the most sought-after villas are to be found. Further north is Óbuda, and to the south, beyond Gellért hegy (Gellért Hill), is the rather bleak suburb of Kelenföld; beyond that is an area half developed for the World Exhibition (planned in the 1990s) which was later abandoned.

Districts of Pest

Central Pest is divided by two boulevards, unofficially known as Kiskörút (Little Ringroad, running laterally from Margit híd to Szabadság híd) and Nagykörút (Greater Ringroad, running in a wider arc from Margit híd to Petőfi híd). The fifth district is enclosed by the Little Ringroad and contains the major sights, although some lie between the two boulevards. Further east are the City Woodland

Impressions

Park (Városliget), the sports stadia of Istvánmező, and the Kerepesi temető (Kerepesi Cemetery, *see pp54–5*).

BUDA

Gellért Hill and the small plateau of the Buda Castle with its adjacent town rise on the west bank of the Danube. Between the plateau and the river is a narrow strip of land settled since the Middle Ages and known as Víziváros (Water Town). To the north is Óbuda (Old Buda, *see p28*).

Gellért hegy (Gellért Hill)

This dolomite rock (235m/771ft high) was the earliest inhabited part of Budapest. In prehistoric times, cave-dwellers took advantage of the hot springs bursting through a geological fault – springs that still supply the Gellért spa today. In Roman times, the surviving Celts lived in this area, some 2km (1¼ miles) from the military and civil settlements of Aquincum to the north. Nowadays the hill is an agreeable park (*see p58*) with footpaths winding up to the Freedom Monument and Citadella on the summit. The grotto chapel (just above the Gellért Hotel) has been reconsecrated, after being walled up by the Communists (who, incidentally, located their command bunker, for use in the event of Armageddon, in the bowels of the Gellért rock).

Várhegy (Castle Hill)

The town and fortress of Buda only achieved real significance in the second

The church of Krisztínaváros from Castle Hill

half of the 10th century. Of the four ancient royal and religious centres in Hungary – Székesfehérvár, Esztergom (*see p122*), Veszprém and Buda – the last to develop was Buda. An economic boom in the 11th and 12th centuries led to the expansion of Buda, Óbuda and Pest, and an increase in religious foundations. The Tartar invasion of 1241 devastated the whole region, but thereafter King Béla IV, known as the refounder of the nation, encouraged settlers from abroad and built the first fortress on Buda Hill.

The rise of Buda

The basic layout of the town of Buda, which has endured until today, dates from the last third of the 13th century, when the two-storeyed Gothic houses for wealthy burghers were built. Buda had two communities: the Germans, whose Church of Our Lady (later the Matthias

Church) stood to the south; and the Hungarians, whose Church of Mary Magdalene was at the northern end.

The first Anjou king, Charles Robert (1308–42), chose to build his great palace upstream of Buda at Visegrád (*see p123*), and it was not until 1347 that Louis I ('the Great') moved his court to Buda and major expansion of the Royal Palace began. Sigismund of Luxembourg (1387–1437) built a lavish new palace in the 15th century and invited masters from Paris, Stuttgart and Augsburg to decorate it. The apotheosis was reached under Matthias Corvinus (1458–90), whose Italian masons and craftsmen created the most glittering royal court in contemporary Europe.

Decline and restoration

After the Turkish conquest of 1541, churches were vandalised and turned into mosques; Buda slowly decayed until its liberation by Habsburg troops in 1686, though the reconquest itself left most of the town in ruins. Subsequently, a small baroque Buda grew up, together with a very plain and functional baroque palace, erected under Maria Theresa.

In the late 18th and early 19th centuries, high-ranking officials lived in Buda and the Diet (parliament) met there (for the last time in 1807). While Pest expanded rapidly, Buda stagnated, although areas bordering on Castle Hill, such as Krisztinaváros and Rózsadomb, became desirable residential areas. The last rebuilding of the Royal Palace took place after the 1867 Ausgleich (Compromise) with the Habsburgs that created the Austro-Hungarian Empire. Subsequently, Buda was destroyed by the Russian siege at the end of World War II and rebuilt in the 1950s and 1960s as a showcase of historic restoration.

Descending from Várhegy (Castle Hill)

PEST

The origins of Pest lie in the Roman period, when a small fortress to protect the ferry crossing at the narrows was built at what is now the Pest end of the Erzsébet híd (Elizabeth Bridge). In the late 10th century traders settled near the ferry to exploit the Danubian ship traffic.

In the 11th century a burial chapel for St Gellért was erected, the first sanctuary on the site of the Belvárosi plébániatemplom (Inner City Parish Church, *see p52).* The unfortunate missionary had in fact been about to cross from the Buda side when he was intercepted and drowned in the river by supporters of the pagan faction (1046).

Poet Attila József sculpted in brooding pose

Shortly afterwards (1061), the first documentary mention of the town of Pest appears.

Medieval and baroque Pest

In the 11th and 12th centuries, Pest expanded to become a substantial and wealthy trading town, with a royal residence, a Dominican cloister and a parish church. After the Tartar invasion of 1241, King Béla IV renewed its privileges as a Royal Free Town, but many of its mainly German inhabitants moved to the comparative safety of Buda. In the 14th century, it boomed again under the Anjou dynasty, when the parish church was enlarged and altered to the form of a *hallenkirche* (hall church).

After the Turkish occupation (1541–1686), building began again in Pest; a hospital for war veterans was built by Italian architects in 1716, together with several baroque convents and churches (for example, those of the Servites, the Franciscans and the Hungarian order of Paulites). Of the baroque palaces built by aristocrats, few traces remain; Andreas Mayerhoffer's Péterffy Palace (1755) in Pesti Barnabás útca (now the Százéves restaurant) is a rare example.

Expansion

Pest came into its own in the 19th century. In 1805 János Hild presented his plans to improve the city to the Embellishment Commission supported by the Palatine. The proposed parks and public buildings were to be financed by selling building plots and by the revenues of customs and local taxes. The inner city (Belváros) thereafter became a largely residential area with churches and schools. Neighbouring Lipótváros (Leopold's Town) was the business centre, increasingly also the domain of wealthy assimilated Jews. Neoclassical buildings – the Magyar Nemzeti Múzeum (National Museum), the Calvinist and Lutheran churches – gave the city its monumental character up to the revolution against the Habsburgs of 1848, when many neoclassical dwellings were destroyed.

In the second half of the 19th century, Pest became the hub of a rapidly expanding and industrialising capital. Whereas in 1850 the populations of Buda and Pest were roughly equal, by 1900 only one in six Budapestians lived in Buda. The great boulevards crossed by the radial of Andrássy útca were now built, as were three new bridges. Miklós Ybl located magnificent neo-Renaissance palaces along the streets and designed a graceful opera house (1884). Theatres, museums and hotels, many on a grand scale, enriched the cityscape of Pest. The monumental Szent István bazilika (St Stephen's Basilica) was begun in 1851 and the even more grandiose Országház (Parliament) was completed just after the turn of the century. The Millennial Celebrations of 1896 put the seal on all this dynamism and self-confidence, while the idiosyncratic buildings of Ödön Lechner (*see pp66–7*) and his school gave expression to the Magyar soul in architecture.

From the 20th century onwards, Pest has begun to sprawl into suburbia, but at its heart is still the bustle and business of that dynamic 19th-century city, now reawakening to capitalistic enterprise, artistic creativity and gourmet refinement.

The Parliament (Országház) as seen from Buda

THE ANCIENT TOWN OF ÓBUDA

The Roman province of Pannonia was created in the 1st century BC and divided by Trajan into Upper and Lower Pannonia around AD 106. Aquincum (*see pp92–3*) was the civil capital of Lower Pannonia. Close to it was the military *castrum* (camp), at the Óbuda end of Árpád híd (Árpád Bridge), and its associated domestic buildings known as *canabae*.

Two of the chiefs of the seven Magyar tribes (Kende and Kurszán) took up residence in Óbuda, and the

Fő tér in Óbuda

first church – a burial chapel built over the grave of the paramount chief, Árpád – was raised in Óbuda at the end of the 10th or the beginning of the 11th century.

In the Middle Ages, the town increased in wealth and importance, particularly under Béla III, who entertained Frederick Barbarossa here in 1189. A Cistercian cloister was built, and other religious orders followed in the 14th century, when the widowed queen of King Charles Robert of Anjou moved her palace to the town. Under Sigismund of Luxembourg, Óbuda even boasted a university (founded in 1389, the first in Hungary).

Like Buda and Pest, the town suffered under the Turkish occupation, but in the 18th century the Habsburgs bestowed the Óbuda lands on the Zichy family. They built their great mansion close to Fő tér (*see p35*), and encouraged Jews to settle, thus boosting the area's economy. Crafts and trade received further stimulus in the 19th century when Count Széchenyi founded the shipyard on Óbuda Island and the Goldberger textile factory began operations (both now closed).

Sadly, Óbuda has suffered from the ravages of time and Communism. The once picturesque provincial town is now a concrete jungle with a few isolated pockets of Roman and baroque charm and elegance. A visit to these relics (and the delightful local museum at Kiscelli) will give a hint of past glories.

The Royal Palace as viewed from the Gellért Monument

Walk: Szabadság híd to Ferenciek tere

This is one of two walks exploring the historic core of Pest. It begins just outside the former old city wall (follow the route in green on the map below; for orange route see p32).

Allow about an hour.

Start at the Pest side of Szabadság híd (see p41).

1 Corvinus Egyetem (University of Economics)

The former Karl Marx University at Fő vám tér 8 was one of the more liberal institutions under Communism. Miklós Ybl's building (1874) was originally the Customs House. Its grandeur reflects Pest's importance as a centre of trade in the late 19th century.
www.corvinusegyetem.hu

2 Központi Vásárcsarnok (Central Market)

Behind the university is the largest of Pest's five market halls (*see p143*), opened in 1897 as a spin-off from the 1896 Millennial Celebrations.
Walk east along Vámház körút as far as Kálvin tér.

3 Református templom (Calvinist Church)

This rather plain neoclassical church (*see p55*) took 14 years to build due to funding problems. Inside is the tomb of Countess Zichy.

From Kálvin tér it is a few minutes' walk on Múzeum körút to the Magyar Nemzeti Múzeum (Hungarian National Museum, see pp72–3). Otherwise turn left into Kecskeméti útca, or make a short detour to Ráday útca, which is a pedestrian zone on summer weekends.

4 The Old City Wall

The post-modern Hotel Korona stands on the site of the city gate. Just beyond the archway is an inscription: '*Itt állt a középkori pesti városfal*' ('Here stood the medieval city wall of Pest').

5 Jogi Kar and Egyetemi templom (Faculty of Law and University Church)

Further along the street on your left is the elegant neobaroque Faculty of Law and adjoining it the University Church (1742, *see pp52–3*), probably the work of Andreas Mayerhoffer. In the early 19th century it was a centre of the reform movement.
Turn left down Szerb útca.

6 Szerb templom (Serbian Church)

You now come to the pretty Serbian Church (*see p57*) built by the Serbian community in 1698. It is said that at the beginning of the 19th century every fourth house in Pest was owned by a Serb merchant.

Retrace your steps to Károlyi Mihály útca.

7 Károlyi palota (Károlyi Palace)

Károlyi Mihály útca 16 was the city residence of Count Mihály Károlyi, first president of the Hungarian Republic in

1918. His widow, known as the 'Red Countess', kept an apartment here. Today it houses the Petőfi Museum of Literature (*see p75*).

8 Egyetemi Könyvtár (University Library)

At the end of Károlyi Mihály útca is the south side of Ferenciek tere (Square of the Franciscans). At No 10 is the University Library, an impressive neo-Renaissance building (1876).

Buses leave from Ferenciek tere and there is also a metro stop for the blue line.

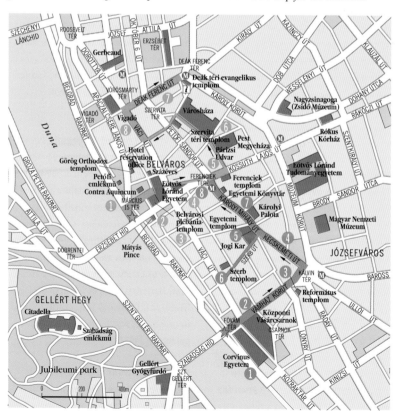

Walk: Erzsébet híd to Deák Ferenc tér

The walk begins at the Roman fort where Pest originated, and includes the fashionable shopping area of Váci útca. See map on page 30, following the route in orange.

Allow 1 hour.

Start in front of the church at Március 15 tér at the Pest end of Erzsébet híd (see p41).

1 Contra Aquincum

This diminutive fortress (*see p92*), with walls 3m (10ft) thick, was a 4th-century outpost in barbarian territory that protected the main town of Aquincum on the far side of the river.

2 Mátyás Pince

If you want to experience a typical (if touristy) Hungarian restaurant with gypsy music, cross under the bridge to the Mátyás Pince at Március 15 tér 7, an institution since it opened in 1904.

3 Belvárosi Plébániatemplom (Inner City Parish Church)

The most historic church of Pest (*see p52*) is on Március 15 tér. It has had an eventful history: the Romanesque and Gothic churches were both largely destroyed, while the Turks turned the diminished building into a mosque.

Highlights of the mostly baroque interior are the two lovely Renaissance tabernacles made of red marble.

A detour to the north takes you to the Görög Orthodox templom (Greek Orthodox Church) at Petőfi tér 2 (drop in to hear the singing at 6pm on Saturdays).

4 Eötvös Lóránd Egyetem (Lóránd Eötvös University)

Named after the distinguished physicist (1848–1919), this is Budapest's main university and was originally a Piarist 'gymnasium' (secondary school). You pass under the building's connecting archway on your way to Kigyó útca and thence to Ferenciek tere. In the parallel Pesti Barnabás útca, at No 2, is the Százéves (100 Years) restaurant, located in one of the few remaining baroque palaces of Pest.

5 Párizsi Udvar (Paris Arcade)

Flanking Ferenciek tere to the north is the striking Jugendstil (art nouveau) arcade designed by Henrik Schmahl (1911), with its oriental-looking stained-glass cupola. The arcade is undergoing changes with shops dedicated to holograms and books interspersed with vacant lots and a hip café. Jégbüfé, on Ferenciek tere, is a good place to stop for light refreshments before carrying on across Kossuth Lajos útca to the Ferenciek templom (Franciscan Church, *see p53*). On the north wall is a relief showing Count Wesselényi rescuing Pest inhabitants by boat during the floods of 1838.

Take the next street left after Petőfi Sándor útca.

6 Pest Megyeháza, Városháza (County and City Halls)

The Pest County Hall (No 7 Városház útca) is a simple neoclassical building (1830), while the City Hall (Nos 9–11) is an elegant baroque structure designed by Antonio Martinelli in 1735 as a hospital for the war-wounded. It was established by Emperor Charles VI. An imposing Atlas bearing a globe stands over the entrance.

7 Szervita tér (Servite Square)

The street leads to the square which was recently renamed after the Servite Order, whose church (1725) stands on the corner (*see p57*). Two recently restored Jugendstil houses (*see pp68–9*) at Nos 3 and 5 are worth a glance, especially the mosaic in the gable of No 3, which is a florid representation of 'The Transfiguration of Hungary'.

The statue of Vörösmarty, rich in detail

Turn left into Petőfi Sándor útca, right immediately into Régiposta útca, where the folkart craftsman's shop is pinpointed by a copper peacock above the door, then right again into Váci útca.

8 Váci útca to Vörösmarty tér/Gerbeaud Cukrászda (Coffee House)

This fashionable shopping area (a pedestrian zone) is always bustling with people. On the square is the monument to the poet Mihály Vörösmarty (1800–55). At the north end is the celebrated 1870 Gerbeaud coffee house and confectioner's, with its enticing menu of Viennese and Hungarian pastries (*see p169*).

The metro junction, where the three lines meet, is located nearby at Deák Ferenc tér to the east.

Walk: Óbuda

High-rise blocks have ruined this once delightful area, but there are still a few pockets of historic interest and charm that make this a lovely walk.

Allow 2 hours, or 3 hours if the Kiscelli Múzeum is included.

Take bus No 86 from Batthyány tér to Nagyszombat útca, or the HÉV railway to Tímár útca, and walk back south.

1 Amfiteátrum

This vast Roman arena was built for the military in the 2nd century and could accommodate 15,000 spectators.

According to the medieval German epic *Das Nibelungenlied*, Attila the Hun ruled from 'Etzilburg', sometimes identified with this amphitheatre.

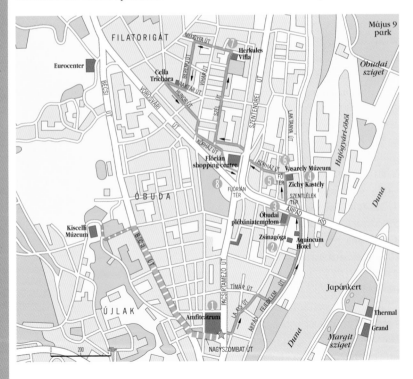

A longish detour via Nagyszombat útca and Bécsi útca is required for the Kiscelli Museum (*see p71*).
Bear right along Lajos útca and right again along Tímár útca. You emerge on a green sward bordered by Lajos útca and Árpád fejedelem útja.

2 Zsinagóga

The fine neoclassical building of this former synagogue at Lajos útca 163 was designed by András Landherr in 1825 for the growing Jewish community.

3 Óbudai plébániatemplom (Óbuda Parish Church)

In front of the church (*see p55*) is a lawn and chestnut avenue lined with sandstone statues. It stands on the site of the Roman military camp. The tomb of Count Peter Zichy, who was given the lands of Óbuda by the king, following the expulsion of the Turks, lies beneath the pulpit inside the church.
Cross under Árpád Bridge to Szentlélek tér and Fő tér.

4 Zichy Kastély (Zichy Mansion)

The baroque family home of the Zichys was built in 1757 by Henrik Jäger. It contains the Lajos Kassák Memorial Rooms, dedicated to Hungary's greatest avant-garde artist and writer. Adjoining it is the Vasarely Museum with art by Hungarian-born Viktor Vasarely.

5 Fő tér

The delightful main square of Óbuda is flanked by baroque houses. At No 4 is a collection of folk artefacts and at No 1 the Óbudai Múzeum.

6 Imre Varga's Sculpture

At the corner of Laktanya útca is *Strollers in the Rain*, Imre Varga's sculpture of ladies with umbrellas.
Pass beneath Szentendrei útca and bear right to the Herkules Villa.

7 Herkules Villa

Covered in a blue awning, the Herkules Villa, at Meggyfa útca 21, evidently belonged to a well-to-do Roman. From the same period are the remains of a rare *cella trichora* (clover-leaf chapel) at the junction of Hunor útca and Raktár útca. (*See also p93.*)
Continue to Flórián tér.

8 Flórián tér

The underpass and adjacent park area have many Roman pieces on show.
Trams run to Pest, or return to Szentlélek tér, for buses to Buda and Pest.

Zichy Mansion (Kassák Múzeum)
Tel: (06 1) 368 7021;
www.museum.hu/budapest/kassak.
Open: Tue–Sun 10am–6pm. The Zichy Mansion also houses the **Óbudai Múzeum** (*tel: (06 1) 250 1020). Open: Tue–Sun 10am–6pm.*
Vasarely Museum *Tel: (06 1) 388 7551;*
www.vasarely.tvn.hu. Open: Tue–Sun 10am–5.30pm.
Zsigmond Kun Collection (Lakasmúzeum)
Tel: (06 1) 386 1138. Open: Tue–Fri 2–6pm, Sat–Sun 10am–6pm.
Imre Varga Collection *Tel: (06 1) 388 6771. Open: Tue–Sun 10am–6pm. Admission charge.*

Baths of Buda and Pest

Of Budapest's many public baths, the four described here all have good facilities, interesting historical features, and architectural charm. The general website for the Budapest baths is: www.budapestgyogyfurdoi.hu

Gellért Gyógyfürdő (Gellért Spa)

The Buda spa most popular with visitors is where the earliest inhabitants exploited the mineral springs of the Gellért Hill; later, the poor of Buda bathed here (and watered their horses) during the Turkish occupation.

The present establishment goes back to a decision of the City Council in 1901 to purchase the land and exploit the springs, whose outlet had been covered over when the Szabadság híd (Freedom Bridge) was built in 1896. Plans for a hotel and spa were finally approved in 1909. The building was completed and opened in 1918.

The architecture is in an agreeably over-the-top version of Jugendstil. The main indoor pool presents a fantasia of mosaics, columns and gargoyles. The entrance hall recalls the grandiosity of the Caracalla Baths in Rome.

Kelenhegyi útca 2–4. Tel: (06 1) 466 6166. Open: Oct–mid-May Mon–Fri 6am–6pm, Sat–Sun 6am–4pm; mid-May–Sept Mon–Fri 6am–7pm, Sat–Sun 6am–7pm (pool), 6am–5pm (spa); July–mid-Aug Fri & Sat 8pm–midnight

The wave bath of Buda's most popular spa, the Gellért

(with music). Admission charge. Tram: 47, 49 and bus: 7, 7A (from Pest); Tram: 18, 19, 41, 48 and bus: 86 (from Buda).

Király Gyógyfürdő (King Spa)

The bath, built by Pasha Mustapha Sokollu, was completed in 1578. There was no thermal spring nearby, so water was piped from the Lukács area.

The bath had several owners after the reconquest of 1686, the last (1796) being a certain Ferenc König (Király in Hungarian), from whom it takes its name. The charming neoclassical wing was added in 1826 and the hydraulic system was renewed in 2007.

Fő útca 84. Tel: (06 1) 202 3688. Open: for men, Tue, Thur & Sat 9am–8pm; for women, Mon, Wed & Fri 7am–6pm. Last entry one hour before closing. Closed: Sun. Admission charge. Metro: Batthyány tér.

Lukács Gyógy-és Strandfürdő (St Luke Spa)

Under the Turks, the spring here was used to drive a gunpowder mill, although a hospital spa named after St Luke had occupied the site of the present baths in the Middle Ages.

Lukács is an oasis of calm and charm with its huge courtyard in the shade of ancient plane trees. The clientele is intellectual and professional, and gossip as important here as bathing.

Frankel Leó útca 25–29. Tel: (06 1) 326 1695. Open: Mon–Sat 6am–7pm, Sun 6am–5pm. Admission charge. Tram: 17 (from Buda).

Rudas Gyógyfürdő és Uszoda (Rudas Spa & Turkish Bath)

Rudas' centerpiece, the Turkish bath, was built in the 16th century during the Turkish occupation. The stunning 10m (33ft) dome is supported by eight pillars, underneath which is the octagonal pool that has been a men-only enclave since 1936. Today, however, women are allowed to use the pool on Tuesdays, and weekends are a mixed bag – when swimsuits are compulsory.

Döbrentei tér 9. Tel: (06 1) 356 1322. Open: daily 6am–6pm. Turkish vapour bath open: Mon–Fri 6am–8pm, men only (except Tue women only); Sat & Sun 6am–5pm, mixed; Fri & Sat 10pm–4am, mixed, with music. Admission charge. Tram: 18, 19; bus: 5, 7, 8, 86 to the Buda bridgehead of Erzsébet híd.

Széchenyi Gyógyfürdő (Széchenyi Spa)

The most impressive spa on the Pest side opened in 1913 (enlarged in 1927). It is a rambling neobaroque establishment supplied by a thermal spring discovered in 1876. The water rises from a depth of 1,256m (4,120ft) at a temperature of 70°C (158°F).

Állatkerti körút 11 (in Városliget). Tel: (06 1) 363 3210. Open: daily 6am–7pm (last entry 6pm) and until 10pm in high summer. Admission charge (deposit system, part of it returned depending on length of stay, keep receipt carefully). Metro: Széchenyi Fürdő.

Spa city

The spas of Buda and Pest evoke memories of a leisured age

In the prehistory of Buda, hundreds of spring-fed streams trickled off the hills into a riparian swamp, and thence into the Danube. When the Celtic Eravisci arrived, they occupied the Gellért Hill and, probably, other parts of the west bank. When the Romans took over they retained the picturesque name the Celts had given to their settlement – Ak-Ink, meaning 'Abundant Waters' – and Latinised it to Aquincum.

There is still a Római fürdő (Roman bath) near the ruins of Aquincum, one of three fed by a source at nearby Csillaghegy. It seems that the Magyars, too, exploited the waters, for the newcomers divided Buda into areas known as Felsőhévíz (Upper Thermal Waters) and Alsóhévíz (Lower Thermal Waters).

In the Middle Ages, at least two hospitals based on spas were founded (at today's Gellért and Lukács baths) by the Knights Hospitallers of St John. For the Turks, bathing had a ritual significance; between 1541 and 1686 numerous Turkish baths were built; they remain today as almost the sole architectural and cultural legacy of Ottoman rule.

Budapest was officially designated a spa city in 1934 by the International Spa Congress (which subsequently moved its headquarters to the city). It certainly deserves the title, for there are 123 springs in Buda, Óbuda and Pest, spouting an estimated 70 million litres (15.4 million gallons) of water daily and supplying 47 baths, of which 12 have extensive medical facilities. The water temperature varies between 24° and 78°C (75–172°F). Many of the springs are sulphurous or slightly radioactive: they are used to treat rheumatism, circulation disorders and gynaecological complaints.

Budapest baths have something for everybody: there are open-air and sports pools, artificial wave baths and bubble baths, medicinal and mud baths, warm, cool and Turkish baths. All those pounds put on from consumption of heavy Magyar dishes can (theoretically) be lost again in the city's 'abundant waters'.

Bridges

In 1870, when Gusztáv Zsigmondy was carrying out a survey of the Danube, he discovered, just north of today's Árpád Bridge, the sunken piles of a wooden Roman bridge. This was the first and only Budapest bridge until the 19th century (see pp98–9).

Although Sigismund of Luxembourg and Matthias Corvinus seem to have planned stone bridges in the 15th century, nothing came of their projects. A pontoon was in operation by the beginning of the 16th century; Turkish engineers subsequently built a more sophisticated 70-drum version, roughly where the Elizabeth Bridge is now.

After the reconquest, an ingenious so-called 'flying bridge' was put into operation by the enterprising Viennese. It consisted of a catamaran that was attached to the banks by long ropes resting on barges. By manipulating the rudder, the boat could be made to swing from shore to shore, using the force of the current. It was in use until 1790, by which time an elegant 'swaying promenade' with 43 pontoons had been built. Opened at dawn and midday, it had to be dismantled in winter because of ice-floes. The municipal authorities would bed safe paths across the ice with straw, charging users double the pontoon toll (nobles, soldiers and students went free). During a big freeze, fairs and balls would be held on the river. The last ball (in 1883) ended in tragedy when the ice suddenly gave way, tipping the dance floor into the glacial waters and drowning 40 people.

Building and naming bridges

Since the first of Budapest's bridges in modern times was completed in 1848, nine more have been built within the city boundaries to relieve traffic congestion in the centre. The vicissitudes of history are reflected in the various name changes: today's 'Liberty Bridge' was planned as 'Customs House Square Bridge', but inaugurated by the emperor himself as 'Franz Joseph Bridge'. The 'Chain Bridge' later became 'Széchenyi Chain Bridge' in honour of its originator, while 'Petőfi Bridge', to the south, bore the name of the interwar regent Miklós Horthy for a while.

The Árpád Bridge to the north was officially 'Stalin Bridge' in the 1950s, and reverted to its original name after the 1956 revolution. All Budapest's bridges had to be rebuilt after the war, as they were blown up by the retreating Germans.

The new Lágymányosi híd to the south takes its name from the Buda district of Lágymányos.

Erzsébet híd (Elizabeth Bridge)

The 290m (951ft) suspension bridge was built between 1897 and 1903 and reconstructed to a modern design after World War I. Its structure weighs just over 1,000 tonnes, but carries 29 90-tonne components of carriageway. Building it entailed wholesale destruction of the medieval core of Pest – the Old Town Hall was demolished and the Inner City Parish Church only escaped thanks to vociferous popular protest.

Bus: 5, 7, 7A, 8, 78, 112.

Margit híd (Margaret Bridge)

A French engineer, Ernest Gouin, designed the second bridge to be built (1876) after the Chain Bridge (*see pp98–9*). To keep its two sections vertical to the current (divided here by Margaret Island) there is a 30-degree angle at the apex. A supplementary ramp (1900) leads down to the island.

Tram: 4, 6; bus: 6, 26, 91, 191.

Szabadság híd (Freedom Bridge)

An all-Hungarian effort in design and construction, this iron console bridge was inaugurated by Emperor Franz Joseph in 1896. The silver spike he ceremonially struck into the Pest abutment was stolen during the 1956 revolution. The Hungarian coat of arms is displayed on the central arches, topped by the mythical turul bird, supposed begetter of the Árpád dynasty.

Tram: 47, 49.

Overview of Széchenyi Chain Bridge

Walk: Tabán and Gellért hegy

On this walk the self-confident architectural elegance of the 19th century is interspersed with glimpses of a turbulent past.

Allow 2 hours.

Begin at Clark Ádám tér, reached by buses 16 and 105 from Pest or 86 along Fő útca on the Buda side.

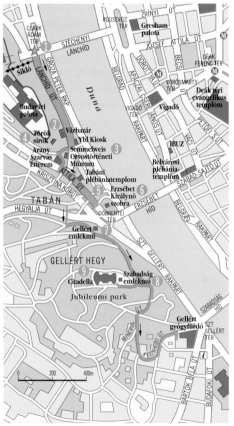

1 Clark Ádám tér

The square, situated at the western end of the Széchenyi lánchíd (Chain Bridge, *see pp98–9*), is named after the bridge's Scottish builder. The northern side is flanked by two fine blocks made by Miklós Ybl (1814–91). In front of the funicular railway (*siklò*) up to the castle is the kilometre stone, whence all distances from the capital are measured.

Walk 100m (110 yds) along the Lánchíd útca. On your right you come to the Várbazár.

2 Várbazár

This once elegant, now decayed, complex of steps and terraces was designed by Miklós Ybl to link the castle with the Danube shore. Across the street is a statue of Ybl in front of the Kiosk (now the Vákert Casino, *www.vakert.com*), which he built in neo-Renaissance style to camouflage the castle's water-pumping station.

3 Semmelweis Orvostörténeti Múzeum (Semmelweis Museum of Medicine)

At Apród útca 1–3 is the neoclassical house of the Museum of Medicine (*see p76*), named after the discoverer of puerperal fever, who was born here.

4 Török sírok (Turkish Graves)

Take the steps leading up between the museum and another Ybl-designed house where Adam Clark died.
From here walk back southwards, passing the Aranyszarvas Étterem (Golden Stag) restaurant in a simple baroque building.

5 Tabáni plébániatemplom (Tabán Parish Church)

The Tabán was a lively area of pubs and traders until its demolition in 1930. The parish church of St Catherine survives at Attila útca 11.

6 Erzsébet Királynö szobra (Statue of Queen Elizabeth)

South of the church is the monument to Emperor Franz Joseph's wife, the pro-Hungarian Elizabeth of Bavaria. A plaque recalls that the previous monument on this site, to the pro-fascist politician Gyula Gömbös, was blown up by the Communist resistance in 1944.
Make your way under the spaghetti junction to the steps at the foot of the Gellért Hill.

7 Gellért emlékmű (Gellért Monument)

A stairway leads to this memorial (*see p95*) to the missionary St Gellért (Gerard of Csanád), allegedly martyred here. There is also a scenic waterfall.

8 Szabadság emlékmű (Freedom Monument)

The steep climb to the top of the hill is rewarded with stunning views. On the summit is the Freedom Monument (*see p96*). The heroic Russian soldiers have been removed, leaving only an allegorical female figure and pieces of the permanent exhibition of military history.

9 Citadella (Citadel)

Above the monument is the Citadella, built by the Austrians in 1854 as barracks and fortress from which to keep a vigil on the unruly inhabitants of Budapest. It now has shops, a restaurant, a hotel and viewing terrace.
Descend through a pleasant park to the Gellért spa (gyógyfürdő) and the buses and trams on Szent Gellért tér.

Statue of Queen Elizabeth

Walk: Tabán and Gellért hegy

Walk: Margit sziget

Margit sziget (Margaret Island) is Budapest's loveliest park, with a history stretching back to Roman times. Originally it was three islands, the largest of which (Rabbit Island) was for long a royal hunting estate. Margaret was the daughter of King Béla IV. She retreated to a convent here in 1252, when only nine years old.

Allow 1¹/₂ hours.

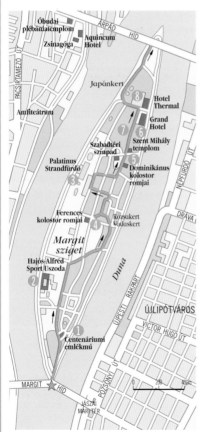

The walk begins at the southern end of the island, reached by bus 26 from the east side of Margit híd (Margaret Bridge). Alight at the first stop on the island or take tram 4 or 6 to Margit híd.

1 Centenáriumi emlékmű (Centennial Monument)

The large fountain, colourfully lit at night, was erected in 1972. It commemorates the centenary of the unification of Buda, Pest and Óbuda in 1872–3. A large restaurant, terrace, casino and stage are on the right.

2 and 3 Hajós-Alfréd Sport Uszoda and Palatinus Strandfürdő

Serious swimmers can enjoy the massive indoor pool of the Hajós Baths, named after the gold medallist at the 1896 Athens Olympics. Hajós was also a successful architect and designed the pool and the building in 1930. On the way to the Palatinus open-air baths and slides (which have a mechanism for making artificial waves), you pass the attractive Rózsakert (Rose Garden) on your right.

4 Ferences kolostor romjai

Between the baths is a ruined Franciscan church dating from 1272. Palatine (Viceroy) Joseph's splendid villa built next to the chapel in 1796 was destroyed in the 1838 flood. The Archduke encouraged development of the island's spa and laid out gardens, but the public were not allowed in until 1869. There is a small zoo with birds of prey as well as chickens, deer and more (*open mid-Apr–Oct 10am–6pm tel: (06 1) 474 2220*).

5 Dominikánus kolostor romjai/Szabadtéri színpad

Northeast of the Palatinus Baths are the ruins of the Dominican convent where St Margaret lived a life of daunting asceticism (even washing was viewed with suspicion). Not far to the west is a water tower you can climb and an open-air stage used for opera performances in summer.

6 Szent Mihály templom (St Michael's Church)

To the northeast is the reconstructed Romanesque church of St Michael, which was built in 1930 using materials from the original 12th-century Premonstratensian church (the ruins of the Premonstratensian convent are nearby). In the church is a 15th-century bell, discovered in 1914 under a tree

St Michael's Church

that had blown down in a storm. The monks had probably buried it before the arrival of the Turks to prevent it being melted down to make cannon.

7 Sculpture Avenue

Along the promenade to the Grand Hotel are busts of Hungary's greatest painters, poets and musicians. Among them is the 19th-century poet János Arany, who liked to sit under the island's trees in the evening composing his romantic lyrics.

8 Grand Hotel, Hotel Thermal

Further north is the beautifully restored Grand Hotel designed by Miklós Ybl, a true reflection of a more leisurely age. Beyond it is the ugly Hotel Thermal; to the west the charming Japanese Garden. *At the northern end of the island, bus 26 can be boarded again either to Árpád híd metro (Pest side) or to Nyugati pályaudvar metro via Margit híd (Buda side). Otherwise climb Árpád híd for bus 106 to Óbuda-Aquincum or Árpád híd metro (Pest side).*

Walk: Rózsadomb and Víziváros

At the turn of the 20th century, elegant villas were built on the Rózsadomb (Hill of Roses), while the Víziváros (Water Town), so called for being constantly flooded, was settled by craftsmen and fishermen in the Middle Ages.

Allow 2½ hours.

Start from the western end of the Margaret Bridge (Margit híd) and make your way to Frankel Leó útca via Vidra útca.

1 Lukács Gyogy-és Strandfürdő and Malom-tó

At Frankel Leó útca 25–27 is the Lukács spa (*see p37*) with a pleasant tree-shaded courtyard. Across the street is a ruined Turkish gunpowder mill and a millpond (Malom-tó). If you walk through to the back of Lukács and turn left, you can see the Turkish Császár Bath, built by Pasha Sokollu in 1570. *Turn up a cobbled street at the junction of Török útca and Frankel Leó útca. Turn left up the steps.*

2 Gül Baba türbéje

This tomb of a famous Dervish scholar (*see pp53–4*) is reputedly the northernmost Muslim shrine in Europe. It is customary to remove your shoes before entering. There is a lovely view of Pest from here. *Climb up to the junction of Gül Baba útca and Vérhalom útca. Make your way down Apostol útca to Rómer Flóris útca, across Margit körút and along Fekete Sas útca.*

3 Bem szobor
(József Bem Monument)

The Polish general Bem fought for the Hungarians in the 1848 War of Independence.

4 Flórián kápolna

The baroque chapel of St Florian (1760) is nearby at Fő útca 90; peer through the glass entrance to see the frescoes and a finely carved pulpit.

5 Király Gyógyfürdő

These baths (*see p37*) were built for the garrison under the Turkish occupation. In the dimly lit interior the play of light beams in the rising steam is an aesthetic experience. The baths are a centre of the Budapest gay scene.

6 Öntödei Múzeum
(Foundry Museum)

A sign next to the baths points to this unusual, wooden-roofed museum. The exhibits deal with metal working from the Bronze Age to that of steel.
Bem József útca 20. Tel: (06 1) 201 4370; www.omm.hu/ontode. Open: Tue–Sun 9am–5pm.
Return to Fő útca and continue south past the grim military prison (Nos 70–74) and Nagy Imre tér.

7 Batthyány tér

The Szent Erzsébet templom (Church of the Elizabethan Nuns) is on your left, just before the square. Their charitable tradition is maintained in the old people's home now occupying their convent. On the right is the rococo inn, at the Sign of the White Cross, behind which the post-chaise used to leave for Vienna. Szent Anna templom (St Anne's Church, *see p56*) is to the south. Next to it is the Angelika coffee house, sometimes described as the favourite rendezvous for the 'society of old hens'.

8 Batthyány tér to Clark Ádám tér

Further along Fő útca is the Szilágyi Dezső teri templom (Calvinist Church) designed by Samu Pecz, whose statue stands beside it. Beyond it is the former Capuchin Church (No 32), remodelled in the 19th century. Opposite the neoclassical No 20 is the graceful post-modernist Francia Kultúra Intézete (French Institute, built in 1992).
Buses for Pest and Buda leave from Clark Ádám tér nearby.

Statue of General Bem

Budavári palota

Royal Palace

Following the devastating Tartar invasions of 1240–41, King Béla IV decided to fortify the southern part of the Buda plateau, since the 11th century a defenceless agrarian settlement and part of Minor Pesth (Lesser Pest).

The castle remained modest until Louis the Great of Anjou moved his court here from Visegrád, probably in 1347. His successor, Sigismund of Luxembourg (1387–1437), built a new palace known as the Friss Palota (New Palace). Sigismund, son of Charles IV of Bohemia, scoured Europe for first-rate craftsmen whom he could lure to Buda. Various engineering projects were undertaken under Sigismund, including the building of a horse-driven pump to supply the palace with Danube water. He was also responsible for placing the vast chain across the river so as to ensure that before merchants went elsewhere they gave the people of the city a chance to buy their goods and thus earn an income for the city.

The golden age

The golden age of the court at Buda was that of King Matthias Corvinus (1458–90): his chapel was equipped with a water organ and his marvellous Bibliotheca Corviniana had 2,000 illuminated codices fastened to lecterns with golden chains. An army of craftsmen made beautiful ceramic stoves for the winter quarters, carved marble fireplaces and doorways, and gilded the coffered ceilings of sleeping chambers. Foreigners were duly impressed. An Italian wrote: 'In all Europe the three most beautiful cities are Venice on the sea, Buda on the hill and Florence on the plain.' Matthias's

PALACE APPROACH

The Royal Palace can be approached from Szarvas tér in the south, reached by buses 86 (Buda side) and 5 or 78 (from Pest). Leaving the Southern Rondella on your right, you pass through the Ferdinand Gate, close to the menacing Mace Tower. Access to the entrance to the Budapest History Museum is via walled gardens.

From the north the palace may be reached using the *sikló* (funicular railway) from Clark Ádám tér, by bus 16 from Pest (Erzsébet tér, Deák F tér metro), or by taking the *várbusz* (minibus) from Moszkva tér.

chief architect was in fact a Florentine, Chimenti Camicia; another great contemporary architect, Giovanni Dalmata (builder of the magnificent cathedral of Sibenik in Dalmatia), also worked for Matthias.

Decay and revival

During the 145-year-long Turkish occupation (1541–1686) the palace fell into decay. In 1678, lightning struck the gunpowder store, causing an explosion that destroyed most of the palace. After the reconquest of Hungary by the Habsburgs and their allies, Charles VI's and Maria Theresa's architects razed much of the Gothic and Renaissance remnants and built a small baroque palace. No longer used as a royal residence – at different times it housed a convent and a university – it was eventually turned over to the Austrian Palatine (Viceroy) in 1790.

After being damaged in the 1848 War of Independence, the palace enjoyed its last flowering after the Compromise with Austria of 1867. Miklós Ybl altered and enlarged the baroque structure between 1869 and 1905. During the interwar period, the so-called Regent of Hungary, Admiral Horthy, installed himself here. In the closing days of World War II, the whole place was reduced to rubble by the Russian bombardment. Though it has since been rebuilt incorporating some relics of the earlier palaces, it lacks the grace and splendour of its predecessors.

Budapesti Történeti Múzeum (Historical Museum of the City of Budapest)

Remnants of the Old Palace

Descend the stairway from the ticket office for a tour through the layers of the Gothic and Renaissance castle. At the entrance are the coats of arms of the Árpáds, the Anjous, Matthias Corvinus and the Jagiellon dynasties.

Highlights include the Renaissance Hall, with a fragment of ceiling by Giovanni Dalmata, an imposing marble fireplace and reliefs of King Matthias and Queen Beatrice. You will also pass an ice-pit connected to the garden above by a chute, and the location of the cistern.

Further on are the former Queen's Quarters and the Royal Chapel of 1380 (the chapel's lower part was rededicated on 18 August 1990 as St Stephen's Chapel). From here you will come to the large, partly Renaissance hall, where concerts are held.

The rear courtyard of the Royal Palace complex, rebuilt after total devastation in World War II

Budavári palota

Gothic statues from the Royal Palace

A special display has been created for the beautiful Gothic statues unearthed in 1974. They were made during the reign of Sigismund and appear to have been thrown into a builder's trench as rubble.

The statues are dated to the third decade of the 15th century and fall into two categories, profane and sacred. Of the profane, some have lean, elegant features, and could be members of the Anjou dynasty with their ladies, and contemporary knights and bishops. Others in this category are foreshortened, suggesting that they were placed high up; they have rounder, more typically Magyar features. Figures in the sacred series have been identified as apostles or prophets.

The striking quality of these works is eloquent testimony to the wealth of Buda in the late Middle Ages, which could afford to employ the best European masters.

Late-Gothic triptychs in the Hungarian National Gallery

History of Budapest

The rest of the museum is a rather old-fashioned exhibition concerning the history and development of Buda and Pest from the Neanderthal period to the Romans (second floor) and from the Romans to the Magyar conquest (first floor). For the subsequent history of Budapest, you should visit the excellent Kiscelli Museum in Óbuda (*see p71*).

Magyar Nemzeti Galéria (Hungarian National Gallery)

The National Gallery and its 70,000 pieces were moved to the reconstructed Royal Palace in 1975. Only Hungarian works (or those executed in Hungary) are displayed here (European masters and other antiquities may be found in the Museum of Fine Arts, *see p76*).

Permanent displays

• Medieval and Renaissance sculpture, including relics of the old Buda and Visegrád palaces – ground floor.
• Gothic wooden sculpture and panel painting from the 14th and 15th centuries, mostly from Upper Hungary (now Slovakia) – ground floor.
• Late-Gothic triptychs, including a celebrated *Annunciation* (1506) by Master MS – first floor.
• Baroque art, dominated by Austrian artists who gained commissions in Hungary in the wake of the Counter-Reformation – first floor.
• Hungarian painting and sculpture of the 19th century. Look out for the charming Biedermeier genre and

MUSEUMS IN THE PALACE COMPLEX

WINGS A, B, C, D:
Magyar Nemzeti Galéria (Hungarian National Gallery) *Open: Tue–Sun, all year round 10am–6pm. Admission charge (free on Sat). www.mng.hu.* For English-speaking guide: *tel: (06 20) 439 7326.*

WING E:
Budapesti Történeti Múzeum
Open: Mar–mid-May & mid-Sept–Oct, Wed–Mon 10am–6pm; mid-May–mid-Sept, daily, 10am–6pm; Nov–Feb, Wed–Mon, 10am–4pm. Admission charge. www.btm.hu.
For the topographical and 19th-century part of the Budapest History Museum, see Kiscelli Múzeum (*p71*). *Tel: (06 1) 487 8801.*

WING F:
Országos Széchenyi Könyvtár
Reading room open: Tue–Sat 10am–8pm. Closed Mon, mid-July–mid-Aug plus select days in Mar, Nov & Dec. www.oszk.hu. Reader's ticket required. *Szent György tér 2. Tel: (06 1) 224 3700.* Guided tours: *tel: (06 1) 224 3745.*

landscape paintings by Miklós Barabás, and the scenes from Hungarian history (works by Gyula Benczúr and Viktor Madarász) – first floor. In another wing (first floor) are Hungarian post-Impressionists and rooms devoted to the most successful Magyar painter ever, Mihály Munkácsy.

• Hungarian painting and sculpture of the 20th century. The highlights here are the dreamlike work of Tivadar Csontváry Kosztka, the pointillism of József Rippl-Rónai and, especially, the output of the *plein-air* artists' colony at Nagybánya. Károly Ferenczy's *October* is perhaps the loveliest picture in the gallery – second floor.

The Palatine's Crypt

Every hour you can join a guided tour to see the vaulted crypt and sarcophagus of the popular Palatine, Archduke Joseph of Habsburg.

Monuments around the Royal Palace

In front of the palace's main entrance is József Róna's equestrian statue of Prince Eugene of Savoy, the hero of the Turkish wars, built in 1900. Emperor Franz Joseph paid for its erection after the town that had commissioned it (Zenta) ran out of money.

To the north is Gyula Donáth's *Turul Bird* (1903), the mythical begetter of the Árpád line of kings. In the western courtyard is Alajos Stróbl's *Matthias Fountain*, a sculptural representation of a ballad by Mihály Vörösmarty, which tells the story of 'beautiful Ilonka', who met and fell in love with King Matthias when he was out hunting incognito. She pined away and died when she realised that her love was hopeless.

Next to the fountain is György Vastagh's lively sculpture showing a *puszta* cowboy breaking in a horse.

Országos Széchenyi Könyvtár (Széchenyi National Library)

The library was founded in 1802 by Count Ferenc Széchenyi, father of the reform politician István Széchenyi. By law it receives a copy of every Hungarian book or journal and also collects scholarly works about Hungary.

Churches and cemeteries

Some of the churches described here are also featured in the different Walks (see pp31, 32 & 35). The historic Matthias Church is dealt with in the section on Castle Hill (see p109).

Belvárosi plébániatemplom (Inner City Parish Church)

The history of Pest is reflected in the many-layered architecture of the *plébániatemplom*. Succeeding a church built on the ruins of Roman Contra-Aquincum, a burial chapel for St Gellért was erected here in 1046. Parts of a subsequent 12th-century basilica survived Gothic reconstruction in the 15th century. The Turks turned the choir into a mosque, as a *mihrab* (prayer niche) in the south wall testifies. Baroque conversion under György Paur was begun in 1725 and two further alterations took place in the 19th century. Twentieth-century restorers have laid bare medieval details such as the sedilia in the sanctuary and the Italian-style 15th-century fresco of the Crucifixion.

The modern panels of the altar, depicting the life of the Virgin Mary, are the work of Pál C Molnár. At the end of the side aisle are two beautiful Renaissance tabernacles in red marble, probably made by craftsmen at the court of Matthias Corvinus. The statue of St Florian recalls fires that badly damaged Pest several times in the early 18th century. (*See also p32.*)
Március 15 tér 2. Tel: (06 1) 318 3108. Metro: Ferenciek tere.

Egyetemi templom (University Church)

It is thought that the Dominicans had a church on this site in the Middle Ages, later turned into a mosque by the Turks. The Hungarian order of Paulites acquired it in the 1720s. Their church was not completed until 1742 (the towers in 1770) and was probably designed by the Salzburg architect Andreas Mayerhoffer.

The rococo ceiling frescoes of the *Adoration of the Virgin* (1776) are by the Bohemian Johann Bergl, while the beautifully carved pews are the work of Paulite monks. The adjacent theological library also contains finely carved shelves and galleries, but may be

difficult to access. (*See also p31.*)
Egyetem tér 5–7/Papnövelde útca. 7.
Tel: (06 1) 318 0555. Metro:
Kálvin tér.

Evangélikus templom
(Lutheran Church)

Emperor Joseph II's Tolerance Patent
(1781) allowed the building of
Protestant churches (but without
towers) in areas where a minimum of
100 Protestant families existed to form
a parish. The Lutheran Church of Pest,
designed by Mihály Pollack, was
completed by 1809 and József Hild
added the neoclassical portico in 1856.
The adjacent Evangélikus Országos
Múzeum (Lutheran Museum) is also
worth a visit: its most treasured
possession is Martin Luther's will,
acquired in 1804. Around 4 per cent
of Hungarians are Lutherans.
Deák Ferenc tér 4. Tel: (06 1) 317 4173;
http://church.lutheran.hu/museum.
Museum open: Tue–Sun 10am–6pm in
summer, up to 4pm in winter.
Metro: Deák Ferenc tér.

Ferenciek templom
(Franciscan Church)

The Italianate baroque church of the
Franciscans in Pest was finished in
1758, but its fairy-tale tower was added
in 1858. The 19th-century frescoes of
the interior are by Károly Lotz. A
marked pew shows where the
composer Franz Liszt used to sit.
Ferenciek tere 9. Tel: (06 1) 317 3322.
Metro: Ferenciek tere.

Gül Baba türbéje
(Tomb of Gül Baba)

The only significant Turkish
monument to survive in Budapest,
other than baths, is the tomb of Gül
Baba, situated in a sunken rose garden
at the top of the cobbled Gül Baba útca
on Rózsadomb.

Gül Baba was a dervish, a luminary
of the Bektashi mendicant order whose
members cultivated the arts and
engaged in agriculture in time of peace,
but were ready to die as martyrs (*ghazi*)
in time of war. He died during a
thanksgiving service for the conquest of
Buda, held in the Matthias Church
(hastily transformed into a mosque) on
Friday 2 September 1541. The Sultan
himself is said to have been among the
pallbearers as this distinguished Islamic
scholar was laid to rest. Hungarians

Inside the Kerepesi Cemetery

later credited him with the introduction of rose cultivation in Hungary. Later still, he entered popular mythology as a harmless figure of fun (he crops up in this role in an operetta by Jenő Huszka based on a story by Mór Jókai). The tomb was built on the orders of the Pasha between 1543 and 1548. It is a modest octagonal building with a hemispherical copper dome topped by a crescent moon.

Originally, this was a place of pilgrimage for pious Muslims and there was also a *tekke* (monastery) next to it. The Jesuits turned it into a chapel in 1689 and kept it until their dissolution in 1773. The Turkish government acquired the shrine in 1885 and donated some of the furniture – the rest has been given by Hungarian Muslims. *Mecset útca 14. Tel: (06 1) 326 0062; www.btm.hu/turbe/turbe.htm. Open: Jan–Apr daily 10am–6pm; May–Sept Tue–Sun 10am–6pm; Oct Tue–Sun 10am–5pm; Nov–Dec daily 10am–4pm. Admission charge. Trams 4 & 6 to Márgit híd budai hídfő, then a short walk uphill or bus 191 from Nyugati pályaudvar metro to Apostol útca, then downhill.*

Kerepesi temető (Kerepesi Cemetery)

Beyond the Eastern Railway Station (Keleti pályaudvar) Pest begins to spread itself with sports stadia, race tracks and the huge (90,000sq m/970,000sq ft) Kerepesi Cemetery. The cemetery, Hungary's national pantheon, is no longer in use. Its status as a patriotic shrine was scarcely enhanced by the inclusion of Communist worthies, buried with full honours traditionally supplied by the unsavoury Workers' Militia. The last to be entombed in the 'Pantheon of the Working Class Movement' was János Kádár in 1989.

Kerepesi Cemetery, last resting place of Hungarian heroes and villains

Perhaps it was the disagreeable company that prompted the son of László Rajk to have his father's remains removed from the area: Rajk Senior (who was just as unscrupulous as his tormentors, but spoke well) was executed after a show trial in 1949, Kádár himself having successfully extracted his 'confession' in prison. His reburial in 1956 after his rehabilitation was attended by 250,000 and lit the fuse for the revolution of that year. Another notable absentee from Kerepesi is Imre Nagy, the ill-fated prime minister of 1956, who was reburied in the Pest Municipal Cemetery in 1989 after a ceremony in his honour on Heroes' Square. Previously, he had lain in an unmarked grave.

Some distance from the burial place of those who enslaved their fellow-countrymen is that of Lajos Kossuth, who led them temporarily to freedom in 1848. The tomb is a rhetorical monument crowned by a figure holding aloft the torch of liberty. Other major public figures who have graves of honour here include Lajos Batthyány (prime minister of the independent government of 1848) and Ferenc Deák (architect of the Compromise with Austria, 1867). József Antall, the first post-Communist prime minister, was buried here, next to Kossuth, on 18 December 1993. The world of the arts is represented by Ferenc Erkel, the actress Lujza Blaha and Zsigmond Móricz (an early 20th-century writer in the Zola mould).
Main entrance in Fiumei útca. Tram: 24 from Keleti pályaudvar (1 stop).

Óbudai plébániatemplom (Óbuda Parish Church)

Károly Bebó is responsible for much of the notable interior of the charming baroque church of St Peter and St Paul in Óbuda. The carved pulpit is especially fine rococo work, with depictions of the Good Shepherd, Mary Magdalene and allegories of Faith, Hope and Charity.
Lajos útca 168. Tel: (06 1) 368 6424.
HÉV: to Árpád híd; or tram 1 to Szentlélek tér.

Református templom (Calvinist Church)

József Hofrichter's rigid neoclassical, somewhat provincial church of 1830 is not much enhanced by the portico added in 1838. The inside is more

Inside Óbuda Parish Church

pleasing, with long galleries by József Hild and stained glass by Miksa Róth, the latter showing Protestant Hungarian heroes and Calvin himself. The treasury contains goldsmiths' work of the 17th to 19th centuries. (*See p30.*)
Kálvin tér 7. Tel: (06 1) 217 6769.
Metro: Kálvin tér.

Szent Anna templom
(St Anne's Church)

The original architect of the city's best-loved baroque church (1761) is unknown, but the design is clearly Italianate. Above the doorway are sculptures representing Faith, Hope and Charity; further up are St Anne with Mary, the Buda coat of arms and a golden eye of God with angels. Inside, note the neobaroque ceiling frescoes by Pál C Molnár (1938) and the graceful pulpit by Károly Bebó.
Batthyány tér 7. Tel: (06 1) 201 3404.
Metro: Batthyány tér.

Szent István bazilika
(St Stephen's Basilica)

Budapest debtors say 'I'll settle up when the Basilica is finished', an allusion to the 54 years (1851–1905) it took to build the church. After the dome of the neoclassical original collapsed (January 1868), Miklós Ybl rebuilt the church to a neo-Renaissance plan. Franz Joseph, attending the consecration, is said to have cast anxious eyes at the dome, whose previous fall, according to an eye-witness, made a 'horrible roar' and broke 300 windows in the neighbourhood. After Ybl's death, József Kauser completed the work. St Stephen's is not basilical in form, but was granted basilical status by Pope Pius XI on the occasion of the Eucharistic Congress held in Budapest in 1938.

Ybl's replacement dome is one of the most striking features of the interior, 22m (72ft) in diameter and 96m (315ft) high. Leading academic artists of the day contributed to the church's

The baroque Serbian Church

The magnificent dome of St Stephen's Basilica

decoration. Károly Lotz designed the dome mosaics, while Gyula Benczúr painted the popular *St Stephen Dedicating his Country to the Virgin Mary* (south transept). The marble statue of St Stephen on the high altar is by Alajos Stróbl.

The star attraction is the Szent Jobb, claimed to be the mummified right hand of St Stephen (at the end of the passage to the left of the altar). In 1938 it was paraded round Hungary in a gold-painted train, but nowadays its excursions are limited to a circuit of the church on St Stephen's Day (20 August). (*See* Walk *on p82.*)
Szent István tér 1. Tel: (06 1) 317 2859. Metro: Deák Ferenc tér or Arany János útca.

Szerb templom (Serbian Church)

The Serbian merchants and craftsmen of Pest had their own printing house and other institutions, including this attractive baroque church (1698). The architect is thought to have been Andreas Mayerhoffer. The iconostasis dates from 1850. Paintings of scenes from the life of Jesus, the saints and the apostles are by Károly Sterio. (*See p31.*)
Szerb útca 2–4. Metro: Kálvin tér.

Szervita templom (Servite Church)

The Servites, one of the religious orders invited to Hungary during the Counter-Reformation, hung on in Pest, although the City Council once forced them to move, and on another occasion compelled them to rebuild on their own plot in a manner the Council thought fitting to the metropolis. Their church is in a pleasantly harmonious baroque style and contains some fine sculpture, notably János Thenny's statues of St Stephen, St Joachim, St Anne and St Ladislas.
Szervita tér 6. Tel: (06 1) 318 5536. Metro: Deák Ferenc tér.

Gardens and parks

The Gellért Hill is criss-crossed with paths (see pp42–3) that afford fine views, and there are many other green open spaces to enjoy in the city.

Európapark

This pleasant grove lies close to Ostrom útca below Bécsi kapu (Vienna Gate) on Castle Hill. In 1972, 100 years after the unification of Buda, Óbuda and Pest, the mayors from various cities round the world planted trees here.
Várbusz from Moszkva tér to Bécsi kapu tér.

Jubileumi park, Gellért hegy (Jubilee Park on Gellért Hill)

On the southwestern side of the hill, below the Citadella and the Freedom Monument, the Jubilee Park was laid out in 1967 to mark the passage of 50 years since the Russian Revolution. The park is a delightful place for walking.
Gellért hegy is reached by trams 18, 19, 47, 48 & 49. Bus: 86 to Szent Gellért tér.

Margit-sziget (Margaret Island)

Margit-sziget is named after Béla IV's daughter, who retired to a convent here. The Turks found the sanctuary a conveniently secure place to keep the Pasha's harem. Palatine Joseph acquired possession in 1796, built a villa here, and laid out a fine park with a rose garden. In 1869 it was opened to the public and became a favourite excursion area for Budapestians. The Habsburg governors sold it to the city in 1908. (*See pp44–5.*)
Bus: 26 from Nyugati pályaudvar. Tram: 4, 6.

Millenáris park (Millennium Park)

The former industrial area of the Ganz-Fabrik was converted in 2001 to this lovely modern park and exhibition halls – an example of new city development.
Between Margit körút and Marczibányi tér (Buda side) behind the Mammut shopping mall. www.millenaris.hu. Metro: Moszkva tér. Tram: 4 & 6 to Szena tér.

Népliget (People's Park)

This now somewhat decayed park was laid out in the 1860s and much

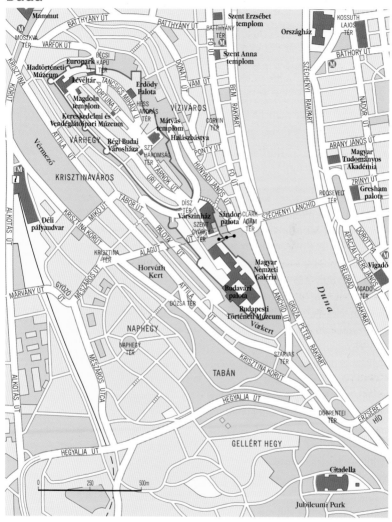

embellished with monuments at the
time of the union of Buda and Pest.
Metro: Népliget.

Városliget (City Woodland Park)

See pp114–15.

Vérmező (Field of Blood)

The leader of the Jacobin conspiracy of
1795, Ignác Martinovics, was executed
here, hence the name. The meadow
covers the site of a medieval village.
Bus: 5 from Március 15 tér.

Hősök Tere

Heroes' Square

The 2.6km (1²/₃-mile) long boulevard of Andrássy útca ends in the east at Heroes' Square, the site chosen at the end of the 19th century for the millennial memorial (see map p64). Every monument on the square relates to the theme of national identity along with the triumphs and catastrophes of Magyar history.

Millenniumi emlékmű (Millennium Monument)

In the vast square that confronts you as you enter from the west, the dominant object is György Zala's 36m (118ft) high Millennium Monument. At the top of an elegant Corinthian column is a representation of the Archangel Gabriel, holding the Crown of St Stephen in one hand and the Apostolic Cross in the other. According to legend, the Archangel appeared to King Stephen in a dream and told him to convert the Hungarians to Christianity. The Apostolic or Patriarchal Cross (with two horizontal bars) signifies King Stephen's role as converter of the nation.

At the base of the column are Zala's romantic representations of the leaders of the seven Magyar tribes who entered the Carpathian Basin in AD 896. The depiction of these fearsome-looking chieftains astride their horses represents the apotheosis of romantic historicism at the turn of the 20th century. In front of the column and the seven chieftains is a simple memorial to the Hungarian soldiers who fell in the two world wars, with a guard of honour on political anniversaries.

The Colonnade

Behind the Archangel Gabriel column is a crescent-shaped colonnade with statues of significant figures in Hungarian history placed above friezes showing crucial historical events. From left to right the statues represent: St Stephen, St Ladislas, Kálmán Könyves (Beauclerc), Andrew II and Béla IV (all of the Árpád dynasty); the Angevin rulers Charles Robert and Louis the Great; János Hunyadi (Regent 1445–52) and Matthias Corvinus; then four Transylvanian princes (replacing Habsburgs); and finally, the 19th-century revolutionary leader Lajos Kossuth (*see p87*). Above are allegorical sculptures of War and Peace, Work and Wealth, Knowledge and Glory.

Pest

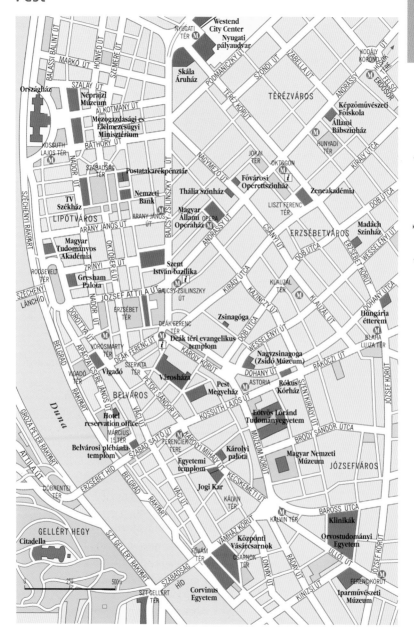

Symbolism and politics on Heroes' Square

After the Ausgleich (Compromise) with Austria in 1867, a degree of sovereignty was at last restored to Hungary after centuries of absolute rule from Vienna. But the fact that the King-Emperor (Franz Joseph) was still a Habsburg posed delicate problems for those constructing a monument to national achievement which, on the one hand, had to make concessions to Magyar pride and, on the other, had to avoid any offence to the ruling house.

Habsburg rule effectively began in 1526 following defeat by the Turks at the Battle of Mohács. In dealing with the period before this, national glory under native and foreign dynasties could be confidently asserted – sometimes providing a salutary historical reminder for the Habsburgs at the same time. An example is the frieze under the colonnade statue of Charles Robert of Anjou which depicts the battle of the Marchfeld (1278); it was here that Rudolf of Habsburg's victory over Ottakar of Bohemia was

Relief of battling Hungarians In Heroes' Square

THE MILLENNIAL CELEBRATIONS

In 1881 the Budapest Council submitted a proposal to the National Assembly for a monument to mark the arrival of the Hungarians in the Carpathian Basin some 1,000 years earlier. Scholars were unable to agree on the exact date of their arrival. In the end, a millennium of 1896 was chosen. György Zala and Albert Schickedanz were given the task of preparing a monumental scheme to celebrate the millennium and 'inspire a sense of continuity and permanence'.

The statues and monuments were actually erected after the millennial celebrations (for which the first stretch of underground railway was also built). The 1896 exhibition celebrating Magyar achievements took up the whole area of the Városliget (*see pp114–15*) and was approached by a triumphal arch on Heroes' Square. It attracted over six million visitors.

secured by the Hungarian king Ladislas IV and his Cumanian cavalry.

Originally the colonnade contained the statues of five Habsburgs: Ferdinand I, Charles VI, Maria Theresa, Leopold II and Franz Joseph himself. These were generally the ones least offensive to Hungarian sensitivities, or even, like Maria Theresa, held in some affection. Under the Communist Republic of Councils (1919), the Habsburg statues were removed and the Millennium Monument turned into a giant obelisk, the front of which featured Karl Marx being fawned upon by grateful workers. Under the Regent, Miklós Horthy, the Habsburgs were returned to their niches, but were once again removed by the Communists after World War II, to be replaced by the independent Transylvanian princes of the 17th and 18th centuries, István Bocskai, Gábor Bethlen, Imre Thököly and Ferenc Rákóczi.

The Rákosi regime would have liked to sweep away the whole monument, since its symbolism was not appropriate to their historical script.

Műcsarnok (Hall of Art)

Schickedanz and Herzog were the architects for the building on the south side of Heroes' Square, the Hellenistic Műcsarnok (1895). It proved useful during World War I, when it was requisitioned as a military hospital. The mosaic on the pediment, *St Stephen as Patron of the Arts*, was a later addition. The gallery mostly shows work by modern Hungarian artists.

Dózsa György útca 37. Tel: (06 1) 460 7000; www.mucsarnok.hu. Open: 10am–6pm except Thur noon–8pm. Closed: Mon.

On the north side of Heroes' Square is the Museum of Fine Arts, devoted to non-Hungarian art (*see p76*). This imposing piece of Hellenistic historicism (1906) was also designed by Zala's co-worker on the Millennium project, Albert Schickedanz, with Fülöp Herzog. *Hősök tere is reached from Vörösmarty tér by the metro (földalatti – yellow line).*

The pantheon of great Hungarians in the Colonnade

Walk: Oktogon to Gundel Étterem

This walk is mostly concerned with the legacy of the Millennial celebrations of 1896, held 1,000 years after the Hungarians first entered the Carpathian Basin.

Allow 2 hours.

Start from the metro station (yellow line) at Oktogon, which is fast food central, and walk east along Andrássy útca.

1 Former ÁVH Headquarters – Andrássy útca 60

The ÁVH, the secret police of the Communist regime, had their headquarters in this building, which they took over from their Nazi counterparts. A plaque on the wall recalls that Cardinal Mindszenty was tortured here. The building is now home to the new **Terror Háza Múzeum** (Museum of the House of Terror, *tel: (06 1) 374 2600; www.terrorhaza.hu. Open: Tue–Fri 10am–6pm, Sat & Sun 10am–7.30pm).*

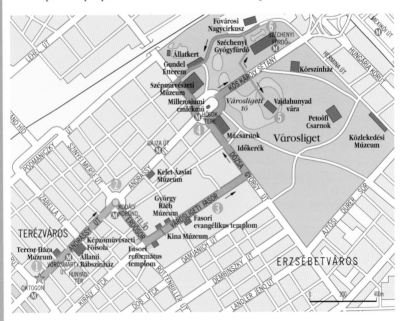

2 Kodály körönd

The roundabout is named after the composer Zoltán Kodály, whose Memorial Museum is at No 1. At each exit of the roundabout are statues of Hungarian heroes of the Turkish wars. *Turn right down Felső erdősor útca and left into Városligeti fasor.*

3 Városligeti fasor

At Városligeti fasor 5–7 is Aladar Árkay's curious **Fasori református templom** (Calvinist Church, 1913), combining Hungarian vernacular with Finnish influence. No less remarkable, at Városligeti fasor 17, is Samu Pecz's neo-Gothic **Fasori evangélikus templom** (Lutheran Church, 1905). Gyula Benczúr painted the *Adoration of the Magi* on the high altar. At No 12 is the **György Ráth Múzeum**, containing Chinese and Japanese artefacts. All along the tree-lined avenue are elegant early 20th-century villas, one of which belonged to the family of the Marxist philosopher György Lukács.
You can rejoin Andrássy útca via Bajza útca, or turn left and walk down Dózsa György útca, passing the area where the Communists held their propaganda rallies.
Note the időkerék (time wheel) behind the Műcsarnok (Hall of Art). It takes one year to make a full turn.

4 Hősök tere (Heroes' Square)

The square (*see p60*) is a national focus of identity created for the Millennial celebrations. On your right is the Műcsarnok, devoted to modern art; on your left is the Szépművészeti Múzeum (Museum of Fine Arts, *see p76*).

The column in the centre of the square is topped by a statue of the Archangel Gabriel.
Beyond Heroes' Square cross the Városligeti tó (lake) on the Kós Károly sétány and turn right down the Vajdahunyad sétány. Rowing boats are available on the lake in summer, and in winter it becomes an ice rink.

5 Vajdahunyad vára (Vajdahunyad Castle)

Ignác Alpár's architectural fantasy (*see p115*) boasts a replica of Vajdahunyad Castle in Transylvania. Other features include a replica of the cathedral at Ják (Western Hungary), the Agricultural Museum and the statue of King Béla III's anonymous chronicler.

6 Széchenyi Gyógyfürdő/ Zoo/Gundel Étterem

Back across the Városliget are the zoo (Állatkert), the Széchenyi Spa (*see p37*), Vidám Park (amusement park) and the lovely Gundel Étterem (restaurant) at Állatkerti útca 2.
The metro (yellow line) leaves from Hősök tere or Széchenyi fürdő.

Zoltan Kodály Memorial Museum
Tel: (06 1) 352 7106. Open: Wed 10am– 4pm, Thur–Sat 10am–6pm, Sun 10am–2pm.
György Ráth Museum
Tel: (06 1) 342 3916; www.imm.hu/fil.html. Open: Tue–Sun 10am–6pm (till 4pm in winter).

Walk: Oktogon to Gundel Étterem

Hungarian national style

'Hungarian form did not exist – but it will now!' With these auspicious words Ödön Lechner (1845–1914) began his idiosyncratic quest for a national style. His remark echoes and complements a similar declaration by Count István Széchenyi in 1830: 'Many people think "Hungary once was": I want to believe "she will be".'

Lechner spent some years abroad, and English and French influences are present in his early work. When Jugendstil/art nouveau arrived in Hungary, he embraced it enthusiastically. In a whimsical interpretation of ethnic roots he happily incorporated Indian, Persian and Moorish motifs, together with ornamentation derived from Hungarian folk art.

Magisterially indifferent to mere technical details of weight or stress, which he left to his long-suffering partners (notably Gyula Pártos), Lechner was equally cavalier about expense – or so his enemies on the city council claimed (in the end they managed to prevent him getting any more commissions). For his part, Lechner pointed out that he used brick, which was cheaper than the stone used by his main rival, and majolica, which was easier to clean. When asked why he ornamented the backs of roofs, which could not be seen, he replied: 'Why shouldn't the birds have something to enjoy?'

LECHNER BUILDINGS
Iparművészeti Múzeum
(Museum of Applied Arts)

The restored Moorish-style stucco of the interior is superb. The stairwell's

Detail from Ödön Lechner's fine Post Office Savings Bank

tiers of undulating carved banisters are topped by an attractive stained-glass cupola.

Üllői útca 33–37. Tel: (06 1) 456 5100; www.imm.hu. Open: 10am–6pm (until 4pm Dec–Mar). Closed: Mon. Metro: Ferenc körút; tram: 4, 6 to Üllői útca.

Magyar Állami Földtani Intézet (Institute for Geology)

Pale yellow walls, strips of brown brickwork and a light blue ceramic roof topped by a huge globe make this one of Lechner's most eye-catching buildings.

Stefánia útca 14. National Geological Museum tel: (06 1) 267 1427. Metro: Stadionok, then trolleybus 75.

Postatakarékpénztár (Post Office Savings Bank)

The walls rise to crenellations of yellow majolica; beyond these is a roof with coloured hexagonal tiles, richly ornamented with floral motifs, angels' wings, dragons' tails and other exotica. The recurrent representations of bee and honeycomb (originally also reflected in the fittings of the interior) symbolise the bank's activity (*see p91*). *Hold útca 4. Metro: Arany János útca.*

Hungarian national style

The Institute for Geology

Jugendstil architecture

In Central Europe the German term 'Jugendstil' is applied to the art nouveau architecture that had its roots in the Paris of the 1890s. In Budapest, the word szecesszió – 'Secession style' – is also used, reflecting the influence of the famous Vienna Secession movement, established in 1897 in opposition to the conservative and academic elements that prevailed in the arts.

Jugendstil/art nouveau was a liberating force, sensual, richly ornamental and prepared to draw eclectically on the world of nature and folklore for its motifs. Coming as it did, with the upsurge of national consciousness in the countries of the Austro-Hungarian Empire, it is not surprising that idiosyncratic versions arose at local level.

Hungarian Jugendstil drew on current ideas about ethnic roots; in the works of Ödön Lechner this was carried further and developed into a so-called 'national style' (*see pp66–7*). However, all Jugendstil architects, whether leaning towards the approach of Lechner, or that of the Viennese Secession, or even that of the English Arts and Crafts Movement, shared a common enthusiasm for exploiting materials such as ceramics, glass and wrought iron; a determination to avoid pattern-book repetition of forms was another characteristic principle. Though in public buildings individuality sometimes had to give way to official or commercial considerations, private villas for the wealthy (of which the vast majority were built at the beginning of the 20th century) provided an opportunity for architects to give free rein to their imagination and ingenuity.

Anyone interested in seeing some of these private houses should spend some time on either side of the outer reaches of Andrássy útca. Examples of fine Jugendstil villas can be seen at Városligeti fasor 24 and 33, both designed by Emil Vidor; further out, at Ajtósi Dürer sor 25, is the villa built for the sculptor György Zala (co-organiser of the Millennium Memorial project), to a modified Lechner design.

Although Ödön Lechner and his partner Gyula Pártos (*see p66*) overshadow the rest, there were many interesting architects in early 20th-century Budapest who built their own more or less idiosyncratic versions of Jugendstil. Their public and commercial buildings are all near the centre of Pest.

Gresham palota (Gresham Palace)

This richly ornamented but crumbling block was built for the English insurance company of the same name by Zsigmond Quittner between 1905 and 1907. It has splendid stairways, stained glass by the Gödöllő artist Miksa Róth, and a marvellous wrought-iron gate with peacock motifs. The palace is now the Four Seasons Hotel.

Roosevelt tér 5. Bus: 16, 105; tram: 2, 2A.

Párizsi udvar (Paris Arcade)

Henrik Schmahl's 1911 arcade has elaborate ornamentation on the façade as well as inside, where the coloured glass lights in the roof create an atmosphere of Alhambra-like mystery.

Ferenciek tere 5. Metro: Blue line to Ferenciek tere.

Török bankház (former Turkish Bank)

The glassed façade of the house (Henrik Böhm, Ármin Hegedűs, 1906) recalls French art nouveau. Miksa Róth made the striking mosaic in the gable, showing the Magyars offering allegiance to the Virgin Mary in her capacity as Patrona Hungariae.

Szervita tér 3. Metro: Deák Ferenc tér.

On the same square, Béla Lajta's **Rózavölgyi Ház** (No 5) betrays the influence of the controversial Viennese architect Adolf Loos. There is another Jugendstil façade at No 2.

Tomb of the Schmidl family

It is worth the long trek to the Jewish Cemetery in Kőbánya to see the loveliest combined effort of Ödön Lechner and Béla Lajta, a gleaming gem of green and turquoise ceramic with gold edging, setting off delicate floral and star motifs. Inside is a stylised mosaic of the Tree of Life.

Izraelita temető, Kozma útca. Tram: 37 (long journey) from Népszínház útca.

The gable mosaic of the former Turkish Bank

Museums

Many of Budapest's more than 40 museums are in buildings of architectural interest, for example, the Ethnographical Museum (see p75). The most important are described here, while others are featured in the Walks. Museums in the complex of the Budavári palota (Royal Palace) are dealt with on pages 48–51. Many museums are closed on Monday and have free admission for the permanent exhibition (but charge for temporary exhibitions).

Bartók Emlékház
(Béla Bartók Memorial House)

The composer Béla Bartók (1881–1945) lived in this villa from 1932 until his escape from Hungary in 1940. In the garden is a life-size statue of him by Imre Varga. Bartók's furniture has been reinstated in the rooms, together with some of his collection of Hungarian ceramics and textiles. The former living room, with its painted wooden ceiling, is used for concerts.

Csalán útca 29. Tel: (06 1) 394 2100; www.bartokmuseum.hu. Open: Tue–Sun 10am–5pm. Admission charge. Bus: 5 to Pasaréti tér, then 10 minutes' walk.

Anyone interested in Bartók's collaborator in the work of collecting Hungarian folk music can visit the Kodály Zoltán Emlékmúzeum (Zoltan Kodály Memorial Museum, *see p65*).

Hardtörténeti Múzeum
(Museum of Military History)

Based in the former Palatine Barracks on Castle Hill, the display includes rooms devoted to the War of Independence (1848–9), World War I and the 1956 revolution.

Toth Árpád sétany 40. Tel: (06 1) 356 9522; www.militaria.hu. Open: Apr–Sept Tue–Sun 10am–6pm (Oct–Mar until 4pm). Admission charge. Várbusz from Moszkva tér to Bécsi kapu tér.

Holokauszt Emlékközpont
(Holocaust Memorial Centre)

Housed in the award-winning new wing of the adjoining Páva Synagogue.

Pava útca 39. Tel: (06 1) 217 6757; www.hdke.hu. Open: Tue–Sun 10am–6pm. Admission charge. Metro: Ferenc körút; tram: 4, 6 to Üllöi útca.

Iparművészeti Múzeum
(Museum of Applied Arts)

The museum was founded in 1872 and was the third museum of its kind in Europe. Its Jugendstil building was designed by Ödön Lechner with Gyula Pártos in 1896 (*see p66*). The opening, attended by Franz Joseph himself, was part of the Millennial celebrations of that year (*see p62*). Its oriental style of ornamentation reflected the architect's view that Magyars had originally come from the East.

Üllői útca 33–37. Tel: (06 1) 456 5100; www.imm.hu. Open: Tue–Sun 10am–6pm (Dec–Mar until 4pm). Admission charge. Metro: Ferenc körút. Tram: 4, 6 to Üllői útca.

Kiscelli Múzeum (Kiscelli Museum)

The most enjoyable of Budapest's history museums chronicles the ages of the city in displays combining nostalgia with scholarship. A section on printing shows the machine that printed Sándor Petőfi's *National Song*, which roused the populace in the 1848 revolution. It is also worth lingering over the paintings, mostly by 19th- and early 20th-century Hungarian masters.

Kiscelli útca 108. Tel: (06 1) 388 7817; www.btmfk.iif.hu. Open: Tue–Sun 10am–6pm (4pm in winter). Admission charge. Tram: 17; bus: 60 to Szent Margit Kórház or 165 to Remetehegyi útca.

Közlekedési Múzeum (Museum of Transport)

The origin of the collection lies in the Millennial Exhibition of 1896 (*see p62*). Features include the history of the Hungarian railway, historic vehicles and urban, water and road transportation.

Városligeti körút 4. Tel: (06 1) 273 3840; www.km.iif.hu. Open: May–Sept Tue–Fri 10am–5pm, Sat & Sun 10am–6pm; Oct–Apr Tue–Fri 10am–4pm, Sat & Sun 10am–5pm. Admission free to the permanent collection, admission charge for the temporary exhibitions. Trolleybus: 70 to Hermina útca; tram: 1 and trolleybus: 72, 74 to Erzsébet királyné útja.

In the **Petőfi Hall** nearby is a permanent display on the history of aviation.

May–Oct, Tue–Fri 10am–5pm, Sat & Sun 10am–6pm; closed Nov–Apr.

The museum has an outlying branch: the **Földalatti Múzeum** (Museum of

Moorish influence in the Museum of Applied Arts

Statue of poet János Arany in front of the National Museum

the Underground Railway) in the Deák Ferenc tér metro station that displays the history of the first underground railway in continental Europe in a disused tunnel section with original vehicles.
www.bkv.hu/muzeum/index.html. Open: Tue–Sun 10am–5pm. Admission charge. Entrance from the pedestrian underpass.

Liszt Ferenc Emlékmúzeum (Franz Liszt Memorial Museum)

The former apartment of Franz Liszt contains photographs and documents illustrating the composer's stormy life (1811–86). Liszt's books, musical scores and much of his furniture have been preserved and there is a bronze of the great man's right hand by Alajos Stróbl.

Vörösmarty útca 35. Tel: (06 1) 322 9804; www.lisztmuseum.hu. Open: Mon–Fri 10am–6pm, Sat 9am–5pm. Closed: 1–20 Aug. Admission charge. Metro: Vörösmarty útca.

Ludwig Múzeum (Ludwig Collection)

This museum contains a collection of contemporary art, donated by the German industrialist Peter Ludwig. It was originally housed in the Buda Castle, but moved to the Művészetek Palotája (Palace of Arts) in the new development Millennium City, where the new Nemzeti Színház (National Theatre) is also situated. The Művészetek Palotája houses the Ludwig Múzeum, the Nemzeti Hangversenyterem (National Concert Hall) and the Fesztivál Színház (Festival Theatre).
Komor Marcell útca 1. Tel: (06 1) 555 3444; www.ludwigmuseum.hu. Open: Tue–Sun 10am–8pm, last Sat of each month 10am–10pm. Closed: Mon. Admission is free to the permanent exhibition, but there is a charge for temporary exhibitions. Tram: 2, 24 to Vágóhíd útca; HÉV: from Boráros tér to Lágymányosi híd.

Magyar Kereskedelmi és Vendéglátóipari Múzeum (Museum of Trade and Tourism)

The emphasis at this museum is on everything to do with the catering and retail grocery trades. The recreated interiors of 19th-century food shops have a great deal of charm, and attractive period posters are on sale. *Szent István tér 15; tel: (06 1) 212 1245; www.mkvm.hu. Admission charge, although permanent exhibition is free. Metro: Deák Ferenc tér or Arany János útca.*

Magyar Mezőgazdasági Múzeum (Agricultural Museum)

This educational museum is another legacy of the millennial show. Of the 18 permanent displays, those on wine production, animal husbandry and fishing are perhaps the most interesting. Horse breeding, also featured, is another field where Count István Széchenyi was active, importing English horses and methods to Hungarian studs and instituting the first horse races. *The museum is housed in the baroque part of the Vajdahunyad Castle on Széchenyi-sziget, Olof Palme sétany, Városliget. Tel: (06 1) 363 1117; www.mezogazdasagimuzeum.hu. Open: Tue–Sun 10am–5pm (Nov–Mar until 4 pm). Admission charge. Metro: to Hősök tere or Széchenyi fürdő; trolleybus: 75, 79 to Hősök tere.*

Magyar Nemzeti Múzeum (Hungarian National Museum)

In 1802, the Széchenyi collection consisted of 11,884 documents, 1,150 manuscripts, 142 volumes of maps and engravings, and 2,675 coins. It was valued at the then enormous sum of 160,000 forints and constituted the

COUNT FERENC SZÉCHENYI (1754–1820)

The story of the Hungarian National Museum begins with Ferenc Széchenyi, father of 'the greatest Hungarian', István Széchenyi, and like him a patriot and moderniser.

Emperor Joseph II appointed him Viceroy of Croatia, but Széchenyi realised that Joseph's centralising and authoritarian approach left no room for national aspirations and resigned his post in 1786. He devoted himself to collecting artefacts and books with a view to donating them to the Hungarian nation; but even this gesture had to receive permission from Joseph's successor, Franz I, before it could be put into effect.

In his old age, Ferenc Széchenyi became fanatically conservative and seems to have suffered from religious melancholy, foreshadowing the mental instability that overtook his son in his final years.

third most important national museum in Europe (after the Louvre and the British Museum). The museum enjoyed the support of the Palatine Archduke Joseph, who became one of the trustees.

Expansion was at first hampered by application of an archaic law under which all objects discovered on Hungarian soil belonged to 'the state' and were transferred to Vienna. Then, in 1832, the great collection of the scholar Miklós Jankovich was acquired, marking the 'second founding' of the museum. At the same time the Palatine persuaded the Diet to allocate half a million forints (to come from the pockets of the nobility) for the construction of an edifice sufficiently splendid to be the repository of the nation's heritage.

Museums

The leading neoclassical architect of the day, Mihály Pollack, was chosen to design the building, which was completed in 1837. Its façade recalls the Erechtheion on the Athens Acropolis, while the interior stairway sweeps up to a domed area reminiscent of the Pantheon in Rome.

The collection

The collection shows the history of the Hungarian people. Highlights include a room devoted to the 1848 revolution, the tent of a Turkish commander and Renaissance stalls with beautiful marquetry from the church at Nyírbátor (northeast Hungary).

Statues on the façade of the Agricultural Museum

ST STEPHEN'S CROWN

In the middle of the Parliament building (*see pp86–7*) is the historic Holy Crown (which actually post-dates the reign of St Stephen). It was returned to Hungary in 1978 from America, where it had been held in safekeeping since the end of World War II.

The crown is that of a Byzantine empress (*corona graeca*) to which an upper part (*corona latina*) was added, perhaps under Béla III (1172–96). The famous leaning cross on the top replaced an earlier one, a reliquary probably containing a fragment of the True Cross.

The *corona graeca* features portraits of the Byzantine emperor Michael Ducas, flanked by his son and the Hungarian king Géza I (1074–7). The precious stones symbolise the four elements – sapphire for air, almandine (a kind of garnet) for fire, green glass for earth and the rim of pearls for water.

The panelled Széchenyi Memorial Room contains a portrait of the founder by the Viennese artist Joseph Ender; round the top of the walls are the coats of arms of all the Hungarian counties.
Múzeum körút 14–16. Tel: (06 1) 338 2122; www.mnm.hu. Open: Tue–Sun 10am–6pm. Admission charge, although permanent exhibition is free. Metro: Kálvin tér; tram: 47, 49; bus: 9, 15, 112, citybusz: 2; trolleybus: 83.

Néprajzi Múzeum (Ethnographical Museum)

This museum is worth visiting to view the neo-Renaissance interior of Alajos Hauszmann's building (1896). It began life as Hungary's Supreme Court, hence Károly Lotz's emblematic fresco on the ceiling, depicting Justitia enthroned among the clouds, flanked by allegories of Justice, Peace, Sin and Revenge.

The first floor is devoted to the traditional culture of the peoples of Hungary and was opened only in 1991. On the second floor, with the help of material from the museum's marvellous photographic archive, primitive cultures are documented, including that of the Ob-Ugrian Hanti and Manszi tribes in the Urals, ancestors of the Hungarians.
Kossuth Lajos tér 12. Tel: (06 1) 473 2400; www.neprajz.hu. Open: Tue–Sun 10am–6pm (4pm Nov–Feb).
Admission charge, but free for permanent exhibitions. Metro: Kossuth Lajos tér; tram: 2, 2A to Szalay útca; trolleybus: 70, 78; bus: 15, citybusz 2.

Petőfi Irodalmi Múzeum (Petőfi Museum of Literature)

Housed in the architecturally stunning and historically important Károlyi palac, this subdued and lovely series of rooms lovingly presents the preserved documents, art, relics and books showcasing Hungarian literature. In addition to Petőfi, Mór Jókai, Attila József and Endre Ady have dedicated exhibitions.
Károlyi Mihály útca 16. Tel: (06 1) 317 3611; www.pim.hu. Open: Mon–Thur 9am–4pm, Fri 9am–3pm.
Admission charge, but permanent exhibitions are free. Metro: Ferenciek tere.

Window in the Ethnographical Museum

Semmelweis Orvostörténeti Múzeum (Semmelweis Museum of Medicine)

Named after Ignác Semmelweis (1818–65), the 'Saviour of Mothers' (*see p43*), whose father had a grocery shop here, the museum has a fascinating display on the history of medicine. There is also a complete neoclassical pharmacy designed by Mihály Pollack. *Apród útca 1–3. Tel: (06 1) 375 3533; www.semmelweis.museum.hu. Open: Tue–Sun 10.30am–6pm (until 4pm Nov–mid-Mar). Admission charge. Bus: 5, 78, 86 to Szarvas tér; tram: 18, 19, 41, 48.*

Szépművészeti Múzeum (Museum of Fine Arts)

This is one of Europe's most substantial art collections, with 2,500 paintings on display, many derived from the Esterházy Collection purchased by the Hungarian state in 1870. The Italian school is particularly well represented with no fewer than five striking El Grecos. *Dózsa György útca 41. Tel: (06 1) 469 7100; www.szepmuveszeti.hu. Open: Tue–Sun 10am–5.30pm (until 4pm Jan–Mar). Admission charge, but free for permanent exhibitions. Metro: Hősök tere; bus: 4, red 4, red 20, 30; trolleybus: 75, 79 to Hősök tere.*

The façade of the Museum of Fine Arts

Music and entertainment venues

One thing that most of Budapest's concert halls have in common is the beauty of their architecture, in particular the Hungarian State Opera designed by Miklós Ybl. This is befitting a country with such a rich musical heritage; Franz Liszt, Béla Bartók and Gustav Mahler are all celebrated here.

Erkel Színház (Erkel Theatre)

Renovation has left little of the building's original Jugendstil ornamentation intact, but its modern styling is itself attractive. In particular, the first-floor buffet area boasts two spectacular wall paintings by the Hungarian painter Aurél Bernáth. At one end is *A Midsummer Night's Dream* and at the other a representation of Imre Madách's Faustian drama *The Tragedy of Man* (1861). Bernáth worked on the paintings between 1972 and 1973.

Köztársaság tér 30. Tel: (06 1) 333 0540. Metro: red line to Blaha Lujza tér.

Magyar Állami Operaház (Hungarian State Opera)

In the 1870s it was decided to build an opera house in Pest of comparable grandeur to those in other European cities. Miklós Ybl won the commission and the opera house went up between 1875 and 1884. Built in a graceful neo-Renaissance style, the technically sophisticated building embodies national pride combined with allusions to musical history. In niches either side of the main entrance are statues of Hungary's two greatest 19th-century composers: Ferenc Erkel (left) and Ferenc (Franz) Liszt (right). Four Muses are represented at the corners of the first storey, while famous composers line the balustrade above. The interior was decorated by Bertalán Székely, Mór Than and Károly Lotz (note Lotz's cupola fresco of Apollo on Olympus). Technical innovations

FERENC ERKEL (1810–93)

First director of the National Theatre, Erkel composed the quintessential Hungarian opera *Bánk Bán* (1861), a musical setting of József Katona's patriotic play about a murder at the medieval Hungarian court. Erkel's music combined elements of the 18th-century *verbunkos* (played on military recruiting drives), folk themes and pre-Verdian opera. He also wrote the remarkably moving Hungarian national anthem (1844).

included new fire precautions, several European theatres having recently burned down with loss of life. It was also something of a feat to install the auditorium's bronze chandelier weighing all of three tonnes. The cost ran to one million forints, most of it personally contributed by Emperor Franz Joseph.

Famous directors of the opera include Gustav Mahler (1888–91), Arthur Nikisch (1893–95) and Otto Klemperer (1947–50). In the 1930s (surprisingly, in view of the right-wing political climate), a number of modern operas were staged, including works by Stravinsky. *Andrássy útca 22. Tel: (06 1) 353 0170; www.opera.hu. Daily one-hour guided tours at 3pm & 4pm; English-speaking guides available. Tours start from the entrance behind the Sphinx. Metro: yellow line (földalatti) to Opera; bus: 4.*

Művészetek Palotája (Palace of Arts)

In Millennium City, this building also houses the Ludwig Collection of contemporary art. Musically, the Bartók Béla Nemzeti Hangversenyterem (Béla Bartók National Concert Hall) has world-class acoustics and can seat 1,700 people. The new concert organ, the largest pipes of which were installed during initial construction, has 92 registers and five manuals. The Fesztivál Színház (Festival Theatre) seats 452 and has similarly excellent acoustics. *Komor Marcell útca 1. Tel: (06 1) 555 3001; www.mupa.hu. Tram: 2, 24 to Vágóhíd útca.*

Pesti Vigadó (The Pest Concert Hall)

Mihály Pollack's original *redoute* (ballroom) on this site fell victim to Austrian cannon fire from the Buda Hill during the 1848–9 War of Independence. Between 1858 and 1865, Frigyes Feszl built a new concert hall in a romantic style that incorporates oriental elements, reflecting the Asiatic roots of the Magyars: one of the figures in the frieze along the top of the façade is Attila the Hun, though the descent of the Hungarians from the Huns is more than doubtful. Further emphasis is placed on Magyar identity by the interior frescoes, scenes from Hungarian folk tales painted by Károly Lotz and Mór Than. 'Vigadó' is coined from *vigad* (to make merry – or have a ball), and the place has never lost its ballroom function (balls are still held here during the Shrovetide Carnival). A free gallery of contemporary art is open Tue–Sun 10am–6pm. Károly Alexy's dancing figures on the façade are thus absolutely appropriate.

Romantic Pesti Vigadó

Vigadó tér 1–2. Tel: (06 1) 354 3755; www.vigado.hu. Tram: 2, 2A along the Pest embankment to Vigadó tér. Closed for renovation until 2009.

Új Színház (New Theatre – formally Parisiana)

This gem of theatre architecture was built as a cabaret venue by Béla Lajta in 1909. Alterations in the 1920s transformed Lajta's original Jugendstil into something closer to art deco. Its complete renovation won it the 1998 Europe Nostra Prize and has resulted in a glittering array of gilding, glasswork and coloured marble.

Paulay Ede útca 35. Tel: (06 1) 269 6021; www.ujszinhaz.hu. Metro: yellow line (földalatti) or bus: 4 to Opera.

Vígszínház (Comedy Theatre)

The charming neo-rococo theatre was built by the Viennese firm of Fellner and Helmer. When it opened in 1896, the public were sceptical of its chances of survival (it was too far out from the centre and had no funding from the state). In fact, a diet of Hungarian and European comedies, played in naturalistic style, soon had audiences flocking to it. Ferenc Molnár was one dramatist who began his career here. Between the wars the staging of modern playwrights' work and visits by guest companies from abroad built up the theatre's reputation.

Pannónia útca 1. Tel: (06 1) 340 4650; www.vigszinhaz.hu. Bus: 6, 15, 26, 91, 191; tram: 4, 6.

Zeneakadémia (Music Academy)

The first music academy was founded in 1875 by Franz Liszt and occupied three rooms above his flat in Irányi útca (Pest); there were then 38 students of piano and composition. After four years, demand was such that expansion became necessary, and the academy moved to Andrássy útca (then Sugár útca), where it occupied several floors and had its first auditorium. At the turn of the century the city decided to buy land for a much bigger music conservatory, subsequently built between 1904 and 1907 to plans by Flóris Korb and Kálmán Giergl.

The Liszt Ferenc Zeneművészeti Főiskola (Franz Liszt High School for Music), to give it its official title, is a remarkable example of Korb and Giergl's idiosyncratic style, sometimes called 'baroque Jugendstil'. Liszt is honoured with a huge statue (by Alajos

---

MIKLÓS YBL (1814–91)

The Hungarian State Opera is probably the finest work of this great Hungarian architect, one of the best practitioners of so-called Historicism.

He built many handsome apartment blocks in Pest, constructed around an internal courtyard, and offered spacious, high-ceilinged flats for the well-to-do. His public works reflect the grandeur and elegance of the Italian Renaissance. They include the second phase of St Stephen's Basilica and the huge Customs House (now the University of Economics). A statue of Ybl stands on the Danube bank below the castle, opposite his Várbazár complex (see p42).

The New Theatre is a dazzling example of art deco

Stróbl) over the main entrance and there are reliefs of two other founding professors, Ferenc Erkel and Róbert Volkmann. The building's exterior is pompous and heavy, but the interior is striking, particularly in the iridescent colours of the Zsolnay ceramic fittings. In the first-floor lobby is Aladár Körösfői-Kriesch's weird fresco *The Fountain of Youth*, with the sententious inscription: 'Those who search for life make a pilgrimage to the wellspring of art.' Its painter was a member of the artists' colony based in the village of Gödöllő, north of Budapest, whose members drew inspiration from Hungarian folk motifs and the English Pre-Raphaelites. Above the entrances to the auditorium on the ground floor Körösfői-Kriesch painted two further frescoes representing sacred and profane music.

The large auditorium of the Music Academy seats 1,200 and is famous for its excellent acoustics. On the walls are images (painted by István Gróh and Ede Telcs) suggesting musical movements – *allegro*, *andante*, *adagio* and s*cherzo*. The smaller auditorium is used for chamber music and seats 400. The foyer has frescoes by János Zichy illustrating Hungarian musical history.

The Academy has had a distinguished past; many world-famous performers such as Antal Doráti, George Szell and Sir Georg Solti are numbered among its pupils. Its professors included all the great Hungarian composers: Ferenc Erkel, Béla Bartók, Zoltán Kodály, Leó Weiner and, of course, Liszt himself. The musical tradition here is unbroken, except for a bizarre interlude at the end of World War II when the building was used for the trial of Ferenc Szálasi, the Hungarian fascist leader and psychopath.
Liszt Ferenc tér 8. Tel: (06 1) 342 0179; www.zeneakademia.hu. Tram: 4, 6 to Király útca; trolleybus: 70, 78 to Teréz körút.

FERENC MOLNÁR (1878–1952)

Molnár made a career on Broadway as well as in his native Pest and is the best-known Hungarian dramatist abroad. His polished and witty comedies are full of psychological insight and erotic innuendo. The Rodgers and Hammerstein musical *Carousel* was based on his play *Liliom* (1909), a low-life story set in the amusement arcade of the City Woodland Park in Pest. Asked how he became a writer, he replied: 'In the same way a woman becomes a prostitute. First I did it to please myself, then I did it to please my friends and finally I did it for money.'

Walk: Andrássy útca

This walk takes you along the grandest boulevard of Pest, with a diversion through theatreland.

Allow 1½ hours.

Walk from the metro stop at Deák Ferenc tér across the east side of Erzsébet tér to the corner of Bajcsy-Zsilinszky útca and József Attila útca.

1 ECE City Centre

Fans of post-modernist architecture will appreciate the reflecting glass and futuristic sculpture of this building (Bajcsy-Zsilinszky útca 12) by József Finta and associates. Finta's work is everywhere – he landed many of the plum contracts for hotels in the Communist period, including the Marriott and the old Taverna (now a Mercure Hotel).

A short detour down Bajcsy-Zsilinszky útca brings you to St Stephen's Basilica (see pp56–7). Otherwise, bear diagonally to the right.

2 Andrássy útca

Originally called Sugár (Radial) útca, the boulevard has reflected political events in its many name changes. It was named Andrássy in 1885 after the distinguished prime minister and foreign minister (1823–90). Under Communism it was first called Stalin Avenue, then briefly Avenue of Hungarian Youth (during the 1956 revolution), then Avenue of the People's Republic, and now Andrássy útca again.

3 Magyar Állami Operaház (Hungarian State Opera)

This is one of Miklós Ybl's most opulent public buildings (*see pp78–9*). Emperor Franz Joseph financed it and attended the opening on 27 September 1884, when Ferenc Erkel's national opera *Bánk Bán* was performed.

Opposite the opera is an early building by Ödön Lechner (see pp66–7), currently undergoing renovation. It will be a hotel. Go down the street opposite it (Dalszínház útca) to Új Színház.

4 Új Színház (New Theatre)

The beautifully restored art deco theatre is worth a visit simply to marvel at the interior (new, but recreated entirely in the spirit of the original).

5 Nagymező útca

Further east on Andrássy útca you come to Nagymező útca, once the

Broadway of Budapest and still boasting several theatres. Turn right down it; at No 8 is the revived **Ernst Múzeum**, containing modern Hungarian and foreign art. The Jugendstil house (*tel: (06 1) 341 4355; www.ernstmuzeum.hu; open: Tue–Sun 11am–7pm*) was partly designed by Ödön Lechner, and the stained-glass window is by József Rippl-Rónai.

Continue down Nagymező útca to the junction with Király útca, where you will see the late baroque Terézváros Parish Church (1809). The open gangway running round the tower was the fire-watch. Inside are two fine neoclassical altars designed by Mihály Pollack. Across the junction at Király útca 47 is the extravagant Pékary-ház (National Savings Bank). Note the

statues of fierce Magyar chieftains over the portals.

Turn left along Király útca until you reach the southern end of Liszt Ferenc tér.

6 Zeneakadémia (Music Academy)

The Music Academy (1907) at Liszt Ferenc tér 8 (*see pp80–81*) is a bizarre mixture of Hungarian national style and eclectic features. Symphonic, chamber and choral works are performed in the auditorium.

Walk north through the buzzing square, passing the modern statue of Franz Liszt (László Marton, 1986) and (at the Andrássy end) a statue of the poet Endre Ady. There is a tourist information bureau at Liszt Ferenc tér 9–11. Turn right on Andrássy útca for the metro at Oktogon.

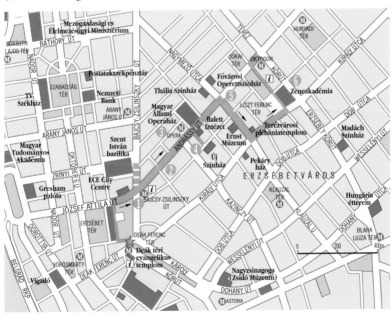

Operetta

Operetta was very popular during the period of the Austro-Hungarian Empire (1867–1918). Its origins were various: Austrian composers were inspired by the smash hits of Jacques Offenbach in Paris and by the tradition of the Wiener Volksstück (Viennese Popular Theatre). The Hungarian equivalent of the latter was the *Népszínmű*. A musical rendering of Sándor Petőfi's poem about the life and love of a peasant boy from the Great Plain (*János Vitéz*) is a classic example of it. The characteristic figures represented in Hungarian *Népszínmű* became the romantic clichés associated with a world that was already passing: the *csikós* (cowboy from the Great Plain), the *betyár* (a sort of Robin Hood), the *huszár* (hussar), the *táblabíró* (provincial judges with feudal attitudes), together with a cast of peasants, *heyducks* (personal gendarmerie of the magnates) and sentimentally portrayed gypsies.

The classic operetta is Johann Strauss's *Die Fledermaus* (1874), a witty and melodious satire on the decadent world of late 19th-century Vienna. The more strait-laced public

The Hungarian State Opera House

Composer Franz Lehár at work

in Budapest were initially slow to accept this, but then came the *Gypsy Baron* (1885), a work that symbolically united the two halves of the Empire. The libretto was based on a story by the greatest Hungarian novelist, Mór Jókai, and Johann Strauss wrote the music. It was an instant success.

The final period of operetta, which was increasingly a vehicle of escape from the realities of imperial decline and war, was dominated by Hungarian composers. Franz Lehár wrote two works that conquered the world – *The Merry Widow* (1905) and *Land of Smiles* (1929). The prolific Emmerich Kálmán had enormous success with the *Csárdás Princess* (1915). The frenetic energy and brittle glamour of its dance routines, set in the nightclub milieu, seem in retrospect to be the dance of death of the Empire itself:

'Every pulse is racing faster
While we dance and flirt and play:
The world outside is all disaster;
What care we till break
of day . . .?'

Országház

Parliament

Feudalism endured in Hungary right up to the 19th century, in some respects even into the 20th. The first glimmerings of modern parliamentarianism are contained in a memorandum submitted to the 1790–91 session of the Diet by a legal historian, József Hajnóczy.

The parliamentary tradition

Leading politicians of the Reform Era (István Széchenyi, Ferenc Deák, József Eötvös) advocated a dilution of noble privilege, and the revolutionary government of 1848 actually raised the proportion of the population enjoying political rights from 2.5 per cent to 8 per cent.

The franchise was effectively narrowed again through tax qualifications in the 1870s and it was not until 1918 that universal suffrage briefly arrived. The Horthy period (partially) and that of Communism (totally) eclipsed democracy, although, in between, free elections were held in 1947. Governments are elected for five-year terms; the next election is due to be held by June 2010.

The building of the Parliament

A competition to design the proposed Parliament building was held in 1883. Only 19 plans were submitted (in contrast to the Berlin Reichstag, which attracted 180 entries); the small number may have been due to the specifications. Imre Steindl (1839–1902) won with a neo-Gothic design, attacked by some as a 'German style', alien to the Hungarians; its supporters pointed out that Magyar and German culture had interacted fruitfully for centuries. In its style, river position and cruciform layout the building showed the influence of Barry and Pugin's new Palace of Westminster on the Thames in London.

The exterior presents a dazzling array of finials, buttresses, towers and a mighty dome. The gilded, marble-clad interior lives up to its role as a national

'If I were the ruler of Hungary, I would order all ships passing by on the Danube to stop for two minutes in front of the Houses of Parliament, so that travellers on board can admire, enjoy and learn from the beauty of the best Hungarian building.'
József Keszler, writing in *Magyar Nemzet* when the Parliament was completed in 1902.

LAJOS KOSSUTH (1802–94)

A provincial lawyer and journalist, Kossuth made his first major political move by founding *Pesti Hírlap*, which (illegally) reported the proceedings of the Diet. He was briefly president of Hungary in 1848, but was forced into exile by the failure of the revolution. The rest of his life was spent abroad – in England, America and Italy, where he died. He remains a potent symbol of the Hungarian struggle for freedom.

2, 2A; *trolleybus: 70, 78; bus: 15, citybusz to Kossuth Lajos tér.*

The Parliament in statistics

One thousand workers took 17 years to build the Parliament. It is 265m (869ft) long, 123m (404ft) wide and 96m (315ft) high (including the dome). It required 40 million bricks and 30,000 cubic metres (over 1 million cubic ft) of stone cladding and has 691 rooms, 17 gates, 29 staircases and 12 lifts. Only 23 years after completion, renovation had to begin, as the stone chosen by Steindl was too soft.

shrine. In the Speaker's Hall is Mihály Munkácsy's vast historical picture showing the Hungarians under Árpád receiving the homage of the Slav tribes of the Carpathian Basin.

You can also see the Hungarian crown in the Parliament building since its move from the Hungarian National Museum.

Statuary around the Parliament

To the south is a statue of the 20th-century poet Attila József, seated overlooking the Danube he celebrated in verse. To the north is Mihály Károlyi, briefly prime minister of a democratic Hungary in 1918. On the square is the 18th-century freedom fighter Ferenc Rákóczi II; and Lajos Kossuth to the north.

Kossuth Lajos tér. www.parlament.hu. Visits with English-speaking guides offered daily 10am, noon & 2pm unless there is a session or ceremonial event. Tours start at Gate X just right of the main stairs. The guards will let you in to buy tickets just 15 minutes before the tour (tel: (06 1) 441 4904). Metro, tram:

Statue of Ferenc Rákóczi II, with Parliament beyond

Országház

Pályaudvarok (railway stations)

The second half of the 19th century saw the building of several iron and glass constructions in Budapest, chiefly market halls and railway stations, inspired by English and French models.

Keleti pályaudvar (Eastern Railway Station)

Budapest's Eastern Railway Station (designed by Gyula Rochlitz and János Feketeházi, 1884) has a 44m (144ft) steel framework behind a rather grandiose, recently renovated neo-Renaissance façade. Two British engineers are honoured with statues high up on the triumphal arch that spans the main entrance: on the right is James Watt (1736–1819), inventor of the steam engine; on the left, George Stephenson (1781–1848), builder of the famous *Rocket* locomotive in 1829.

Despite the station's name, many trains from the west arrive here, just as trains for the north and east leave from the Western Railway Station.

The square in front of Keleti pályaudvar is named after Gábor Baross (1848–92), who was transport minister in the 1880s. He rationalised the Hungarian railway system by nationalising the six existing private railway companies. *Metro: Keleti pályaudvar.*

Nyugati pályaudvar (Western Railway Station)

The first train on the first stretch of railway built in Hungary left for Vác on 15 July 1846 from the wooden predecessor to the present Western Railway Station. The architect responsible for this gracious example of industrial architecture (1877) was a Frenchman, August de Serres, and it was built by the famous Eiffel Company of Paris. In order to ensure that train services were not disrupted during construction work, the new station was built above and around the old one, which was demolished only when the work was complete.

The station has been restored, not quite authentically, since the (nonetheless attractive) blue paint on the ironwork is a post-modernist conceit. The former Royal Waiting Room, built for the arrival of Franz Joseph and Elizabeth when they attended the millennial celebrations of 1896, is in the east wing. Its ceiling features the coats of arms of the Hungarian counties served by trains from this station. To the right of the main entrance a sumptuous restaurant, redolent of the bourgeois comforts of the railway age, still stands … now the most elegant McDonald's in Europe.

Teréz körút 109–111.

Metro: Nyugati pályaudvar.

The Eastern Railway Station

Pályaudvarok (railway stations)

Walk: Deák Ferenc tér to Kossuth Lajos tér

The walk explores the institutional quarter of Pest.

Allow 2 hours.

Begin at Deák Ferenc tér and walk northwest across Erzsébet tér, leaving the international bus station on your right. On your left you will see the Corvinus Kempinski Hotel, and on the corner of Harmincad útca the huge former bank occupied by the British Embassy.

1 Danubius kút (Danubius Fountain)

In the middle of Erzsébet tér is this triple-basined fountain, a copy of Miklós Ybl's beautiful original. The ladies perched on the lower bowl represent Danube tributaries – the Tisza, Dráva and Száva.

Go through the passageway between the buildings on Bécsi útca to the south.

2 József Nádor szobor

Johann Halbig's statue of Archduke Joseph of Hungary stands in the square. The sixth son of Emperor Leopold II, the Archduke was Palatine of Hungary from 1796 until his death 50 years later. He did much to realise Hungarian aspirations and moderate the policies of the Habsburg court in Vienna.

Turn left down József Attila útca and right into Roosevelt tér.

3 Roosevelt tér

The square (*see pp95–6*) is flanked by hotels at the southern end, and the elegant Magyar Tudományos Akadémia (Academy of Sciences) to the north. There are statues of 19th-century statesmen – József Eötvös (who reformed public education), Ferenc Deák (who organised the 1867 Compromise with the Habsburgs) and István Széchenyi (*see p99*). On the east side are the Ministry of the Interior, the Jugendstil Gresham palota (Palace), now a luxury hotel, and an office block known as the Spinach Palace, because of its colour.

Walk along Akadémia útca and turn right down Széchenyi útca, which leads to Szabadság tér.

4 Szabadság tér

The former stock exchange on the west side is now the TV Székház (Hungarian Television Centre); opposite is Ignác Alpár's eclectic **Nemzeti Bank** (National Bank – 1905). Don't miss the Látogatóközpont (Visitor's Centre) of the National Bank (*open: Mon–Fri 9am–4pm, free*). It is not only an interesting exhibition about the history of the forint and a beautiful building, but you can also mint coins, print your own banknote with your photo on it, see your weight in gold forints or euros and lift a gold bar. *Tel: (06 1) 428 2752; www.mnb.hu*

North of that is the Jugendstil American Embassy, where Cardinal Mindszenty took refuge during the 1956 revolution – and remained for 19 years. The statue nearby is of an American general who prevented Romanian troops from looting the National Museum in 1919. Ödön Lechner's marvellous Postatakarékpénztar (Post Office Savings Bank, *see p67*) is round the corner (Hold útca 4). Just to the north is the Batthyányörökmécses (Batthyány Eternal Flame) commemorating the prime minister of the independent government, Count Lajos Batthyány, who was shot on this spot.

Walk on to Hold útca and turn left into Alkotmány útca, which leads to Kossuth Lajos tér.

5 Kossuth Lajos tér

This vast space is dominated by Imre Steindl's Országház (Parliament, *see pp86–7*), the most ambitious construction project ever undertaken in Hungary. From 1885, some 1,000 labourers and craftsmen worked on it for 17 years.

Alajos Hauszmann's Supreme Court (Kossuth Lajos tér 12), now the Néprajzi Múzeum (Ethnographical Museum), and the Mezögazdasági es Elelmézesügyi Minisztérium (Ministry of Agriculture) occupy the southeast side. The statues on the square represent heroes of the struggle for independence. A statue of executed prime minister Imre Nagy stands alone on a small bridge on adjacent Vértanúk tere.

Walk up past the Fehér ház (White House), formerly the sinister headquarters of the Communists. Tram and bus stops are at the Pest end of Margit híd.

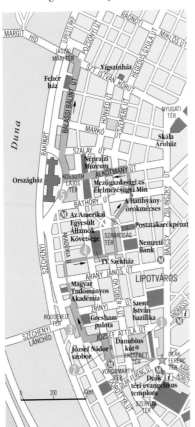

Roman remains

In the 1st century AD *the Romans planted a garrison in the Pannonian Celtic settlement of Ak-Ink ('Abundant Waters') and Latinised the name to Aquincum. An outpost across the Danube was known as Contra Aquincum (see p32). The military camp, on what is now Flórián tér (Óbuda), had its own baths and a huge amphitheatre with seating for 15,000. The civilian town was 2km (1¼ miles) to the north and there were other strategic* castra *and watchtowers, components of the famous defensive system along the Danube known as the* limes.

Aquincum

The town originally existed to service the military – in every sense of the word. Including numerous brothels and pubs, the extensive rest-and-recreation area that surrounded the military *castrum* were collectively known as *canabae*.

At the beginning of the 2nd century Trajan enhanced Aquincum's status by making it the provincial capital of Pannonia Inferior. Hadrian raised it to a *municipium* in AD 124, and in 194, under Septimius Severus, it became a *colonia*. The Roman governor (*legatus*) established his residence on the adjacent Óbuda island.

Aquincum flourished during the 2nd and 3rd centuries, partly due to its proximity to the amber trade route that ran from the Baltic through western Hungary to Aquilea on the Adriatic. Decline set in during the 4th century, at the end of which Rome was forced to make concessions to the Huns and withdraw from the area.

Sights of Aquincum

Substantial ruins of Aquincum remain, indicating the prosperity of a city numbering 40,000 inhabitants who enjoyed the benefits of an efficient water supply, sewage disposal and hypocaust heating. There were warm and cold baths, and houses were decorated with frescoes, mosaics and stucco. In the open-air part of the site are remnants of a forum, law courts, dwelling houses and religious (including Christian) sanctuaries.

The museum contains everyday objects, either made locally or imported via the Rhine and the Danube from Germania and Gaul. Its star attraction is an organ worked by water pressure, a unique survival from Roman times.

Remains around Aquincum

South of the ruins is the so-called Herkules Villa, notable for mosaics depicting the labours of Hercules and Dionysian rites (wine production was encouraged in Pannonia from the 3rd century). One vivid scene shows Hercules about to loose an arrow at a centaur abducting a curvaceous nymph.

Nearby are the remains of a *cella trichora*, an early Christian chapel on a clover-leaf ground plan. It dates to the 4th century and was probably built over a martyr's grave.

Just to the north of Aquincum are the remains of an aqueduct and of the civil amphitheatre, which is only half the size of the military one.

Roman column

Roman remains in Óbuda
Tel: (06 1) 250 1650. Those that are accessible charge admission. See also pp34–5.
An excellent publication in English detailing these sights is *Pannonia Hungaria Antiqua (*Archaeolingua*).*
www.aquincum.hu
The **Amfiteátrum** (Military Amphitheatre), junction of Nagyszombat and Pacsirtamező útca (only exterior view), can be reached by buses 6 & 86 to Pacsirtamező útca.
Aquincum Museum, *Szentendrei útca 139. Tel: (06 1) 250 1650. Open: May–Sept Tue–Sun 9am–6pm (until 5pm in Oct and mid–end Apr; closed: Nov–mid-Apr). HÉV: to Aquincum; bus: 34, 42, 106 from Szentlélek tér, 106 from Árpád híd metro (Pest side).*
The **Cella Trichora** (view from exterior only), at the junction of Hunor and Raktár útca.
Bus: 6, 84, 86; tram: 1 to Flórián tér.
Herkules Villa, *Meggyfa útca 19–21. Tel: (06 1) 430 1081. Open: Oct Tue–Sun 10am– 5pm; May–Sept Tue–Sun 10am–6pm; closed: Nov–Apr. Bus: 6, 86, 118 to Bogdáni útca.*
Military Baths Museum, *Flórián tér 3–5. Tel: (06 1) 250 1650. Open: Tue–Sun 10am–5pm (until 6pm in summer). Bus: 6, 86; tram: 1 to Flórián tér.*
Táborvárosi Múzeum (Roman Camp Museum), *Pacsirtamező útca 63. Tel: (06 1) 250 1650. Open: Tue–Sun 10am–6pm; closed: Nov–mid-Apr.*

Statues and monuments

No free-standing monument from the Middle Ages has survived in Budapest, and most of those of the baroque age have been taken to the Kiscelli Museum in order to conserve them. The striking baroque Trinity Column (1713) on Szentháromság tér is an exception, but even this is largely a post-war replica. It is one of the classic Buda landmarks, on a spot where Masses were held when plague closed the churches.

Today, the visitor sees mainly 19th- and 20th-century statuary, the best of it nobly commemorating men worthy of honour, the worst of it (Socialist Realism) now mostly consigned to the new park of Communist monuments near Nagytétény (*see pp100–101*).

Described here are monuments of historical and/or aesthetic interest. Many others are covered in the Walks or in the descriptions of Kossuth Lajos tér (*see pp90–1*), Hősök tere (*see pp60–3*) or Castle Hill and the Royal Palace (*see pp48–51*).

Anonymus emlékmű (Anonymous Monument)

This is understandably the capital's best-loved monument (1903). The sculptor, Miklós Ligeti, was the beneficiary of money given by Emperor Wilhelm II of Germany, who visited Budapest in 1897 and remarked on the need for more statues in the city. He had in mind more bombastic representations of warriors, but the city

authorities contented themselves with a few muscle-bound Turk-killers on Andrássy útca. Ligeti's subject is very different. Master P was the anonymous monkish chronicler of Béla III, and his *Gesta Hungarorum* (1204) was the first history of the Magyars. The sculptor has respected the historian's anonymity by hiding his face under his cowl.
Courtyard of Vajdahunyad Castle.
Metro: Hősök tere.

Bajcsy-Zsilinszky emlékmű (Bajcsy-Zsilinszky Monument)

The dramatic sculpture (by Sándor Győrfi, 1986) shows the politician who headed the non-Communist resistance to the Nazis at the moment of his arrest in Parliament by Hungarian fascists in 1944. He was shot shortly after his arrest. On the base of the monument is a quotation from Ferenc Kölcsey: '*A haza minden előtt*' (the homeland before everything).
Deák Ferenc tér.
Metro: Deák Ferenc tér.

Gellért emlékmű
(Gellért Monument)

On a dramatic site overlooking the Elizabeth Bridge rises the 6.76m (22ft) bronze statue of Hungary's first missionary. Gyula Jankovics' work (1904) is supposedly situated near the spot where Gellért was either hurled to his death or rolled into the Danube, nailed inside a barrel (versions differ). St Gellért (Gerard Sagredo) was born in Venice around 980 and martyred in 1046. He tutored King Stephen's son Emeric, and was made Bishop of Csanád by King Stephen in 1030.

Bus: 5, 78, 86 to Szarvas tér.

József Nádor emlékmű
(Palatine Joseph Monument)

Johann Halbig's elegant bronze figure (1869), draped in the cloak of St Stephen's Order, honours the younger brother of Emperor Franz I. Archduke Joseph (1776–1847) headed the Embellishment Commission (*see pp114–15*) that transformed the face of 19th-century Pest. He was one of the few Habsburgs to be loved by Hungarians.

Metro: to Deák Ferenc tér, then a short walk to József Nádor tér.

Kodály Zoltán szobor
(Statue of Zoltán Kodály)

In a grove on the northeast slopes of Castle Hill is Imre Varga's remarkable bronze (1982) of the composer Zoltán Kodály (1882–1967), which has been likened to pop art. Varga is a prolific creator of modern public monuments, highly naturalistic, and often with a touch of humour.

Europapark. Várbusz: from Moszkva tér to Bécsi kapu tér.

Raoul Wallenberg emlékmű
(Raoul Wallenberg Monument)

Another bronze by Imre Varga (1987) is a belated tribute to the 'righteous Gentile' who saved thousands of Budapest Jews in 1944 by issuing them with Swedish ID cards. He probably died in a Russian gulag after the war.

Szilágyi Erzsébet fasor. Tram: 56 (four stops) from Moszkva tér.

Roosevelt tér (Roosevelt Square)

The best surviving architectural feature of the square, which was once ringed by fine neoclassical buildings, is the Magyar Tudományos Akadémia (Academy of Sciences) at the northern end. The neo-Renaissance building was designed by a Berlin architect, Friedrich Stüler, and completed in 1861.

St Gellért (Gerard Sagredo), first missionary to Hungary

A statue of István Széchenyi's stands before it; he put up the initial construction funds, with the rest of the money raised from public subscription. On the plinth are figures of classical deities symbolising his multifarious achievements – Minerva, Neptune, Vulcan and Ceres.

Also on the square are statues of Ferenc Deák (*see below*) and József Eötvös (1813–71), who reformed education in Hungary.
Bus: 16, 105 to Roosevelt tér; tram: 2, 2A to Roosevelt tér or Eötvős tér.

Deák emlékmű
(Deák Monument)

Adolf Huszár's monument (1887) honours the lawyer and shrewd politician who was minister for justice in the independent government of 1848–9 and whose Easter Essay in the *Pesti Napló* (16 April 1865) gave the impetus for the political Compromise of 1867 and the setting-up of the Austro-Hungarian Dual Monarchy.

Ferenc Deák was a man of outstanding integrity, who lived for years as a bachelor in a suite of rooms in the nearby English Queen Hotel (the Gresham Palace was subsequently built on the site).
Roosevelt tér. Bus: 16, 105; tram: 2 to Roosevelt tér.

Semmelweis szobor
(Semmelweis Statue)

The marble statue (1906) of the 'Saviour of Mothers', Ignác Semmelweis

(*see also p76*), is by Alajos Stróbl. The sculptor depicted his own wife and baby as part of the ensemble in recognition of Semmelweis's improvements in medical practice that had saved them after a difficult birth.
Rochus Hospital, Gyulai Pál útca.
Metro: Blaha Lujza tér.

Szabadság emlékmű
(Freedom Monument)

As soon as the Russians had 'liberated' Budapest (and Vienna) they hastened to erect monuments in prominent places so that a grateful public should keep their contribution permanently in mind; the Freedom (formerly 'Liberation') Monument (1947) can be seen from most of Pest and much of Buda. Ironically, Zsigmond Kisfaludy-Stróbl's work was originally intended to honour Admiral Horthy's son, a pilot killed in a crash thought to have been engineered by the Germans. The addition of a Soviet soldier holding the red flag and one or two other touches adroitly made the iconographical switch from Horthyism to Communism. The massive female figure holding aloft a palm branch is still there, but the Soviet soldier has gone, following the collapse of Communism.
Gellért hegy. Bus: 27 from Moricz Zsigmond korter, Villanyi útca to the stop Busuló Juhász, and then a 400m (440yd) walk.

Szoborpark (Sculpture Park)

The new home for the city's Communist statuary (*see pp100–101*).

The top of the Great Synagogue tower

SYNAGOGUES
Nagyzsinagóga
(Great Synagogue)

The largest synagogue in Europe is still a centre of liberal Judaism. It was built by the Viennese architect Ludwig Förster (1859) and enlarged in 1931 in Moorish style. Imre Varga's moving weeping willow *Monument to the Holocaust Victims* in the rear courtyard recalls the terrible events of the mid-20th century. The attached Zsidó Múzeum (National Jewish Museum) is situated where Theodor Herzl (1860–1904), the founder of Zionism, was born. It contains disturbing documentation of Jewish persecution.

Balatoni/corner Szabadkai útca (22nd District). Tel: (06 1) 424 7500; www.szoborpark.hu.
Open: daily 10am–dusk. Admission charge. Tram: 19 & 49, or red bus 7 to Etele tér, Kelenfoldi pályaudvar terminus. Then yellow Volánbusz suburban bus on the Budapest–Diósd–Érd line to the Szoborpark Múzeum stop (14-minute journey); buy your ticket at the ticket window or from the vending machine, because Budapest local tickets, day passes and Budapest Card are not valid on the yellow buses (only the new BEB combined 14-day or monthly passes will do). Alternatively, take the Tétény-Busz fast line Mon–Fri from Szent Gellér tér, Budafoki útca or the daily black bus 3 from Móricz Zsigmond Körter, Karinthy Frigyesútca to the shopping mall Campona (the Lépcsős útca stop) and from there bus 50 to the end of the line (Balatoni útca, Szobor Park). Budapest local tickets and passes are valid. There is also an expensive but direct transfer bus from Déák Ferenc tér daily at 11am (also July–Aug 3pm).

Dohány útca 2–8. Museum tel: (06 1) 342 8949. Open: May–Oct Mon–Thur 10am– 5pm, Fri & Sun 10am–2pm; Nov–Apr Mon–Thur 10am–3pm, Fri & Sun 10am–2pm. Closed: Sat.
Synagogue tel: (06 1) 342 1335.
Open: Mon–Fri 10am–3pm, Sun 10am–1pm (except during ceremonies). Closed: Sat. There are combined tickets for the synagogue and the museum. Metro: Astoria or Deák Ferenc tér.

Zsinagóga (Orthodox Synagogue)

The rival to the liberal synagogue was the (moderately) orthodox one, two streets away, which also has a vividly oriental look about it. Currently, the synagogue is under restoration and difficult to visit.
Rumbach Sebestyén útca 11–13.
Metro: Astoria.

Széchenyi lánchíd

Széchenyi Chain Bridge

In 1820, a 29-year-old nobleman was returning hurriedly from Bihar County to Transdanubia for the funeral of his father. He reached Pest on 29 December, only to find that the pontoon bridge over the Danube had been dismantled for three weeks. It was not until 5 January – a full week later – that he could persuade a ferryman to negotiate the treacherous ice floes. The nobleman was Count István Széchenyi and his reaction to this experience was to begin lobbying vigorously for the building of a long-mooted bridge between Pest and Buda.

On 10 February 1832, the Budapest Bridge Association was formed under Széchenyi's chairmanship. Following an old Central European tradition, it included not only enthusiasts, but also those who would otherwise have stymied the project out of jealousy, had they not been included.

Looking through the famous triumphal arches

Opposition came from the municipalities, who were unwilling to forgo the revenue of the pontoon toll, and from the nobility, who clung to their privilege of toll exemption which the owners of a privately built bridge were no longer prepared to indulge. However, the enlightened Palatine, Joseph, supported the project and the resistance of the aristocrats was finally overcome. Széchenyi travelled to England to study bridge-building. He was impressed by William Tierney Clark's suspension bridge at Marlow in Buckinghamshire, and Clark was invited to design the Budapest Bridge. A Scottish master-builder, Adam Clark (no relation), was engaged to supervise the construction work. The project was jointly financed by Viennese bankers (Georg Sina, Samuel Wodianer and Jakob Rothschild). Construction (1842–8) was not without difficulties:

The Chain Bridge – the first to link Pest and Buda

as the last component was being lowered into position, the chain of the hoist snapped, demolishing part of the scaffolding and pitching onlookers (including Széchenyi) into the Danube.

The Chain Bridge was completed just before the outbreak of the War of Independence and survived an attempt by the Austrians to blow it up. It was officially inaugurated after the war (by which time Széchenyi was confined to a Viennese mental asylum). Its imposing triumphal arches instantly became Budapest's most characteristic landmark, but the sculpted lions by János Marschalkó were criticised for apparently lacking tongues. The sculptor was able to demonstrate in several learned articles that lions' tongues 'do not hang out of the mouth like those of dogs'.

The city had given an undertaking to the construction company not to build a competing bridge either side of the Chain Bridge closer than a distance of 8km (5 miles). Pressure of traffic soon made this condition intolerable and in 1870 the municipality bought the company out, so that construction of the Margaret Bridge could begin.

COUNT ISTVÁN SZÉCHENYI (1791–1860)

Called 'the greatest Hungarian' by his political rival Lajos Kossuth, Széchenyi was a reformer, a patriot and an enthusiast for technical innovation. He donated one year's income from his estates towards the foundation of the Academy of Sciences in 1827, and founded, *inter alia*, the National Theatre, the Danube Steamship Company and the Óbuda shipyard. He also organised the regulation of the Danube and the Tisza, and improved the quality of Hungarian livestock.

Although he served briefly as transport minister in the independent government of 1848, his last days were clouded by mental instability. In 1860 he committed suicide in a Vienna sanatorium. His words sum up his political and social attitudes: 'We must struggle for the general good, as well as our own interest.'

Where are they now?

The Communists stamped their presence all over Budapest in the form of street names and monuments, and newly elected city councils have been assiduous in removing these since the toppling of the regime in 1989.

Scores of names have been changed. Many were obvious candidates for oblivion – Engels Square or Lenin Avenue, for instance. Some were names associated with the obsessive Communist quest for legitimacy (Liberation Square, People's Army Square, First of May Avenue); others immortalised little-known minor functionaries.

In the autumn of 1992 work began on the removal (at huge cost) of 56 Communist statues from squares and parks, spurred on by activists of the Hungarian Association of Freedom Fighters of 1956. They announced that if any were left *in situ* on

A statue at Szoborpark

A statue from the Communist era relegated to the Sculpture Park near Nagytétény

23 October (the anniversary of the 1956 revolution), they would tear them down with their own hands – a fate that befell the mega-statue of Stalin during the revolution itself.

Many of the Socialist Realist sculptures have been placed in a specially built park outside Budapest, Szoborpark – a 'Disneyland of old Communism' as the deputy mayor described it. The presentation is dramatic: as you walk through a pedimented gateway flanked by larger-than-life statues of Lenin, Marx and Engels, a vista opens before you of heroically depicted groups of toiling workers or fighting soldiers, powerfully evoking the mixture of ideology and kitsch that passed for Communist art. In the view of the deputy mayor their preservation is itself an assertion of civilised values.

Meanwhile, someone has discovered a warehouse full of Habsburg monuments that miraculously survived destruction in the 1950s. There are, of course, spaces for these now …

For location and details see *pp96–7. www.szoborpark.hu*

Váci útca

Vác Street

Váci útca used to be two streets (it incorporated Lipót útca at the beginning of the 18th century) and they were quite different. However, the southern part, formerly decayed, has been transformed to resemble the pedestrian zone of the northern half. The latter has been likened to shopping centres such as Kärntner Strasse in Vienna or even London's Bond Street.

It was always a fashionable promenade, as 19th-century etchings show, but most of its fine neoclassical buildings have disappeared. Number 9 is the Pest Theatre, built by József Hild in 1840 on the site of a famous hotel and ballroom where the 11-year-old prodigy Franz Liszt once gave a concert. Number 11a is faced with colourful Zsolnay ceramics and was built in the Jugendstil style by Ödön Lechner and Gyula Pártos (1890). Also worth a glance is the post-modernist Taverna Hotel (No 20) by József Finta and Associates (1987) which has just been renovated as a Mercure hotel.

Váci útca seems to be awash with people night and day. There are Transylvanian ladies selling their fine embroidery, tourist tack, high fashion, acacia honey and much else.
Metro: Ferenciek tere or Vörösmarty tér.

Vörösmarty tér (Vörösmarty Square)

The spacious square is entered from Váci útca at a point where the inner city gate for the road to Vác (*see p130*) once stood. Under the trees in the centre is a monument of Carrara marble (by Ede Telcs and Ede Kallós, 1908) to the Romantic poet Mihály Vörösmarty (1800–55). The poet is shown reciting his *Szózat* (Appeal) to the Hungarian masses; etched on the plinth is a line from the poem: 'Be faithful to your land forever, O Hungarians!' Although *Szózat* contains more optimistic passages, the nightmare vision it evoked of *nemzethalál* (national extinction) spoke directly to the hearts of Hungarians, then as now.

On the north side of the square is a block built by József Hild, long known as the 'cutters' house' because a wealthy tailor, a surgeon, a slaughterer and a banker lived here (presumably the banker was seen as someone who could cut off the money supply). On the ground floor is the celebrated café and confectioner's, Gerbeaud (*see p169*).
Metro: Vörösmarty tér.

Váci útca, a fashionable shopping district

Hungarian lifestyle

For centuries Hungary was an agrarian feudal society, and many a city dweller is still provided by country cousins with home-made fare, vegetables and fruit. A popular 'rustic' tradition among young Budapestians today is the *szalonnasütés* (bacon barbecue). In a suitably rural environment, such as Szentendre Island, bacon is roasted with peppers and potatoes, and Magyar folk songs are sung.

A more genuine peasant tradition is the December *disznóölés* (pig-killing); every part of the pig is used to make

Traditional *kolbász*

kolbász (sausage), *hurka* (black pudding), *sonka* (ham), *disznósajt* (pickled feet and ears), *kocsonya* (pork in aspic), *szalonna* (bacon) and *zsír* (lard).

While life in the country is still geared to the rhythm of the seasons, urban Hungarians often juggle their waking hours between two jobs in order to make ends meet. Life is hectic; by Western standards it is also uncomfortable for most, due to a perennial shortage of accommodation. Young married couples are often condemned to live with in-laws, and most families have bedrooms that double as sitting rooms. In the inner city, many live in hideous concrete panel-housing blocks, notorious for their poor quality and lack of privacy. In the suburbs, life is more agreeable for those who live in family bungalows with lovingly tended vegetable gardens. Suburbanites may keep fit by gardening, but city dwellers must turn to other means. Swimming in the spas is a popular pastime, combining as it does opportunities for gossip with healthy exercise. At summer weekends most of Budapest flees to Lake Balaton, where many people have built holiday homes.

More space, more cash and more attention to diet are beginning to have an impact on Hungarian lifestyle. Unlikely to change are the gregarious habits of the Magyars, their capacity to make much out of little, and their ability to fill the calendar with excuses for celebration. Every day, it seems, is somebody's name day, and therefore an excuse for a visit that begins with the enigmatic greeting: '*Isten éltessen sokáig, füled érjen bokáig*' (May God grant you a long life and may your ears reach your ankles).

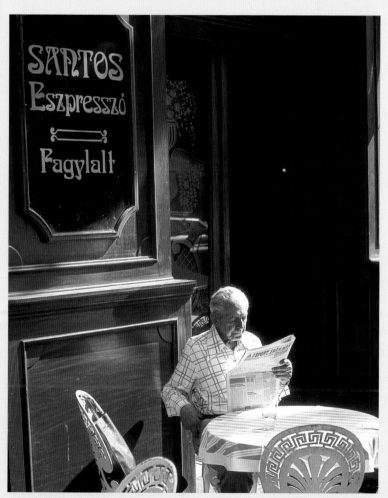

A rare moment to sit and unwind

Várhegy

Castle Hill

The wedge-shaped limestone plateau rising 160m (525ft) on the west side of the Danube consists of the Royal Castle complex (see pp48–51) at the southern end and the ancient town of Buda (the Várhegyed or Castle Quarter), encompassing the middle and northern parts of the plateau.

From the time of Béla IV in the 13th century, old Buda was a residential area ancillary to the court, where retainers, officials, craftsmen and merchants lived (*see pp24–5*). Each component of its mixed population of Germans and Hungarians (also Walloons, Italians and Jews) has left traces here; even the last Turkish pasha has his monument, although there is very little else left to recall the 146-year-long Turkish rule. After the Diet ceased to meet in Buda at the beginning of the 19th century, Pest increasingly eclipsed Buda, until it gradually became the quiet backwater of today.

Access to Várhegy

Whether you want to visit the Royal Palace, the town or both, the following access routes will apply: from the south the approach is on foot from Szarvas tér (reached by bus 86 on the Buda side, buses 5 and 78 from Pest) and brings you through the southern fortifications of the old castle. There are also various flights of steps up from Fő útca in Víziváros (Water Town). The bus from Pest to Dísz tér at the southern end of the Castle Quarter is the No 16 from Erzsébet tér (Deák Ferenc tér metro). The *sikló* (funicular) climbs from Clark Ádám tér at the west end of the Chain Bridge (daily 7.30am–10pm) and arrives at Szent György tér (there is a special fare for this). The *várbusz* (minibus) runs between Dísz tér and Moszkva tér (metro red line) until 11pm; it stops at strategic points in Buda town (city tickets and passes valid).

Bécsi kapu tér (Vienna Gate Square)

To the left of the gate are the sombre State Archives and opposite it is the Lutheran Church containing Bertalan Székely's picture *Christ Blessing the Bread*. There are attractive baroque houses at Nos 5 and 6, and the façade of No 7 is adorned with medallions of Virgil, Socrates, Quintillian, Cicero, Livy and Seneca.

Dísz tér (Parade Square)

The square is flanked by the Water Gate to the east and the Fehérvári or Jewish Gate to the west; to the south are the ruins of the War Ministry. Jews were settled close to the castle by Béla IV and held a Friday market here, until driven out by Louis of Anjou in 1360. Executions (a popular spectacle) were held on the square. In the middle is György Zala's Honvéd Monument (1893), honouring Hungarians who died for freedom in 1848–9.

Fortuna útca (Fortuna Street)

French and Walloon craftsmen lived in the street in the Middle Ages. Gothic elements can be seen in several houses, notably the so-called *sedilia* (sitting niches) in the doorways (for example, at No 5), a unique feature of Buda.

They may have been used by traders for their wares or by servants waiting for their masters.

Halászbástya (Fishermen's Bastion)

Frigyes Schulek designed this neo-Romanesque viewing terrace to the east and south of the Mátyás templom (Matthias Church); completed in 1905, it was named after the Danube fishermen who defended this bastion in the Middle Ages. The conical turrets are supposedly a romantic allusion to the tents of the original Magyar tribes. In front of the bastion is Alajos Stróbl's equestrian statue of St Stephen (1903) holding the (doubled) apostolic cross that symbolises his role as Christianiser of the Hungarians.

Gates to the former Royal Palace

Stained glass at the Matthias Church

The earliest church on this site dates back to the reign of Béla IV (1235–70). It was enlarged in the late 14th century and subsequently added to by Matthias Corvinus, who built the oratory and replaced the south tower that had collapsed in 1384.

During the Turkish occupation it was used as a mosque. Then, between 1874 and 1896, Frigyes Schulek entirely rebuilt it in neo-Gothic style though he stuck to the original ground plan.

In the Middle Ages the Church of Our Lady was where the German burghers of Buda held their services. The kings of Hungary had to be formally accepted by the community in the church following their coronation in Székesfehérvár.

After the Compromise of 1867, Franz Joseph and Elizabeth were crowned in this church, as were the last Habsburgs, Karl IV and Zita, in 1916.

Hess András tér
(András Hess Square)

The square is named after the printer of the first Hungarian book, *Budai krónika* (*The Chronicle of Buda*, 1473) – his printing shop was at No 4. The Hilton Hotel (Nos 1–2) is a modern adaptation of a former Dominican monastery and church. On the St Nicholas Tower of the former church is a copy of a 15th-century Saxon relief showing a triumphant King Matthias. Also on the square is the monument to Pope Innocent XI, initiator of the Holy Alliance formed to reconquer Buda from the Turks.

Kapisztrán tér
(Giovanni Capistrano Square)

Capistrano was a fiery Franciscan preacher who gathered an army against the Turks and took part in the successful siege of Belgrade in 1456.

Appropriately, the Museum of Military History is also on the square (Nos 2–4, *see p70*). On the Anjou Bastion beyond it is the monument to the last pasha of Buda, Abdurrahman Abdi Arnaut (actually an Albanian), who died at his post in 1686.

Protestants (worshipping in the nave) and Catholics (using the choir).
Kapisztrán tér.

Mátyás templom (Matthias Church)

The Church of Our Lady is known as the Matthias Church after King Matthias Corvinus (1458–90), who considerably enlarged and enriched it. The interior was painted with polychrome geometric patterns and frescoes in the 19th century by Károly Lotz and Bertalan Székely; the stained-glass windows show scenes from Hungarian history.

Against the north wall of the choir is the St Ladislas Chapel with a copy of the 14th-century silver bust of the 11th-century saint and king Ladislas I, and frescoes by Lotz illustrating legends about him. In the crypt are grave slabs of the Árpád dynasty. From there, you begin a tour which includes St Stephen's Chapel, painted with scenes from the life of the saint-king, the Royal Oratory (containing Habsburg coronation robes) and the exhibition of ecclesiastical treasures in the north gallery. Below it, in the Trinity Chapel, is the tomb of Béla III and his consort, Anne of Châtillon.
Szentháromság tér 2. Tel: (06 1) 355 5657. Open: 6am–8pm (for groups Mon–Sat 9am–6pm, Sun 1–5pm). English-speaking guides available. Admission charge (also for gift shop). Ecclesiastical history exhibition open: Mon–Sat 9.30am–5.30pm, Sun 1pm–5.30pm.

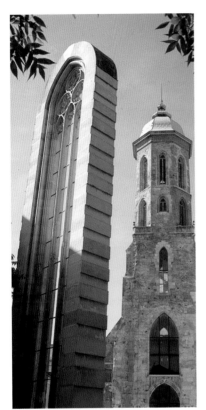
Church of St Mary Magdalene

Magdolna templom (Church of St Mary Magdalene)

The tower and a solitary Gothic window are all that was reconstructed after wartime bombardment of the church. It belonged to the Hungarians in the Middle Ages; after prolonged dispute a borderline between the German and Hungarian parishes had been drawn at the Dominican Monastery (now the Hilton) in 1390. Under the Turkish occupation the church was for a while shared between

Athena guards the old Town Hall, Trinity Square

Nemzeti Táncszínház (National Dance Theatre)

Originally a 13th-century Franciscan monastery, the building was occupied by the Turkish pashas between 1541 and 1686. It was turned into a German theatre in 1787 and saw the first ever Hungarian stage performance in the city on 25 October 1790. Beethoven performed here in 1800.
Színház útca 5–9. Tel: (06 1) 356 4085.

Országház útca (The Street of the Diet)

The Italian craftsmen working on the Royal Palace once lived in this street (it was then called Olasz útca – Italian Street). From the 1780s to 1807 the Hungarian Diet met at No 28, formerly a convent. Of the many attractive survivals, Nos 18–22 retain Gothic and baroque features, while No 2 was a place of some splendour at the time of Sigismund of Luxembourg (note the sitting niches).

Sándor palota (Sándor Palace)

Mihály Pollack and the Viennese Johann Aman designed this imposing neoclassical palace (1805–1821). It was the official lodging of the prime minister between 1867 and 1944 (*see p112–13*) and is now home to the president of the Republic. Note Anton Kirchmayer's frieze on the façade, a mixture of patriotic themes and scenes from antiquity.
Szent György tér 1–2.

Szentháromság tér (Trinity Square)

Trinity Square is the focus of the old town: to the east is the Matthias Church (*see p109*), to the north the neo-Gothic Central Archive (formerly the Finance

Ministry) and to the west the Régi budai városháza (Old Town Hall). This baroque fusion of five Gothic houses was the seat of the council from 1710 to 1873. Szentháromság útca leads off to the west; at No 7 is the Biedermeier café Ruszwurm (*see p169*). In the middle of the square is the Trinity Column (1713) commemorating the abatement of a plague epidemic.

Táncsics Mihály útca (Mihály Táncsics Street)

At No 7 is the baroque Erdődy Palace (1769) housing the Museum of the History of Music. Number 9 may once have been the royal mint; it certainly became the Magna Curia (Royal Court) and was latterly a prison. The writer and agitator Mihály Táncsics was imprisoned here before the War of Independence. The Jewish ghetto was around Nos 21 and 23. Number 26, formerly a synagogue, is now a museum. A wall plan shows the location of Buda's Jewish community at various periods. Dependent on the goodwill of the ruler, they suffered periodic persecution or expulsion. The Christian armies that reconquered Buda in 1686 massacred the Jewish inhabitants, who had established a *modus vivendi* with the Turks.
Synagogue museum: Táncsics útca 26. Tel: (06 1) 355 8849. Open: 10am–6pm. Closed: Nov–Apr.

Tárnok útca (Treasurers' Street)

The name refers to the administrators of the royal monopolies (salt, minerals,

etc) who resided in the area. The street was also the site of a market in the Middle Ages. No 18 is a 15th-century alchemist's lab, which was used as an apothecary's shop from the 18th century. It is now the lovely, though somewhat sinister, Golden Eagle Pharmacy Museum.
Arany Sas Patikamúzeum, Tárnok útca 18. Tel: (06 1) 375 9772. Open: Tue–Sun 10am–6pm, to 4pm Nov–Feb. Free admission.

Úri útca (The Street of the Lords)

At No 9 is the entrance to the cave labyrinth under Castle Hill (*see pp132–3*), while at the junction with Szentháromság útca is an equestrian statue of Maria Theresa's successful Hungarian general, András Hadik, who was also commandant of Buda for a while. His horse is a portrait of a famous stallion from the stud at Bábolna.

Trinity Column and the neo-Gothic Central Archive, Trinity Square

Walk: Várhegy

This walk round Castle Hill gives a flavour of the old town of Buda, painstakingly restored after terrible destruction in World War II.

Allow 1½ hours.

Start from the top of the funicular railway (sikló) that climbs to Castle Hill from Clark Ádám tér.

1 Sándor palota (Sandor Palace)

On your right is the beautifully restored neoclassical former prime minister's

residence (*see p110*). A plaque on the east wall honours Count Teleki, head of the government in 1941, who

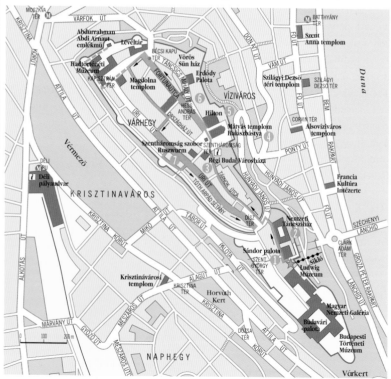

committed suicide here when the decision was taken to allow German troops through Hungary to attack Yugoslavia. It is now the home of the president of the republic.

2 Nemzeti Táncszínház (National Dance Theatre)

The former monastery was converted into a theatre (*see p110*) by the engineer Farkas Kempelen.

Tel: (36 1) 201 4407;
www.dancetheatre.hu
Walk through Dísz tér and Tárnok útca, past the pharmacy museum (see p111), to Szentháromság tér.

3 Régi Budai Városháza (Former Town Hall of Buda)

The early 18th-century town hall on the west side of the square has a pretty bay window; below it is a statue of Pallas Athene, protectress of Buda.

4 Mátyás templom, Halászbástya (Matthias Church, Fishermen's Bastion)

The striking neo-Gothic reconstruction of the Matthias Church (*see p109*) dominates the square's east side, with the Fishermen's Bastion beyond it (by the same architect, *see p107*).

5 Hilton Hotel

Further north, the Hilton Hotel (1976) at Hess András tér 4 was ingeniously designed by Béla Pintér, incorporating parts of a medieval tower, a Gothic church and a baroque seminary.

A detour down Táncsics Mihály útca brings you past the Erdődy Palota (No 7) containing the Museum of the History of Music; next door (No 9) is where leading dissidents were imprisoned before the 1848 revolution.

6 Hess András tér/Fortuna útca

At No 3 on the square is the ancient Vörös Sün-ház (House of the Red Hedgehog – look above the door).

It is worth a detour on to the Anjou bastion to see the monument to the last Turkish pasha (*see p108*). Walk back across Kapisztrán tér to Országház útca, leaving the Magdolna templom (Church of St Mary Magdalene, *see p109*) on your right. On the corner with Petermann bíró útca, note the plaque of 'The Flying Nun'. It recalls the convent of the Poor Clares at Országház útca 28. *Cut through Dárda útca and head south along Úri útca, where there are unusual Gothic sitting niches in the entrance to Nos 31, 32 & 34. After catching the view from the west rampart (Tóth Árpád sétány), turn left by the statue to András Hadik (see p111) into Szentháromság útca.*

7 Ruszwurm

At No 7 is the famous confectioner's (*see p169*). In the late 19th century, Vilmos Ruszwurm's pastries were in such demand that well-to-do Viennese ordered them to be sent by post-chaise. *Turn south out of the street for Dísz tér for bus 16 to Pest; and the* várbusz *to Moszkva tér.*

Városliget

City Woodland Park

The 1km (⅔-mile) square Városliget is a playground for Budapestians, young and old, an historic landmark and a veritable paradise for lovers of trees, of which the park has over 6,900, including several rare species. The area was once a hostile swamp through which meandered the stagnant waters of the Rákos Creek.

In 1240, the Tartar army of Batu Khan inflicted a crushing defeat on the Magyars here by feigning a retreat and luring their opponents on to the marsh. In 1259, Béla IV granted what had now become pastureland, known as the *ukur* (ox land), to the Dominicans of Margaret Island.

The sandy meadows were annexed to Pest by Leopold I, and Maria Theresa instigated systematic tree planting in 1751. The Embellishment Commission of the city further improved the park, after holding a competition (won by a Bavarian landscape gardener, Henrik Nebbien) for the best ideas to beautify it.

The Embellishment Commission

The popular Palatine Joseph threw his weight behind an imaginative 26-point plan for improving and beautifying Pest according to a proposal by the architect János Hild. A commission set up to realise Hild's ideas first met in November 1808. Its primary business

JÁNOS HUNYADI (c.1407–56)

János Hunyadi was Hungary's greatest general in the early wars against the Turks, and the father of King Matthias Corvinus. He was Regent between 1446 and 1453.

Hunyadi rose to prominence at the court of King Sigismund, whose illegitimate son he was rumoured to be. His greatest triumph was at Nándorfehérvár (Belgrade) in 1456, a battle that stopped the Turkish advance for 70 years. To mark this victory Pope Calixtus III ordered the church bells of Christendom to be rung each day at noon in perpetuity.

was urban planning to integrate the city core with fast-developing new districts. The Commission laid down regulations concerning the maximum height of houses and their exterior decoration. It was these that subsequently determined the unified aspect of neoclassical Pest. The Commission also gave its attention to the greening of the city through tree-planting and landscaping of Margaret Island and the City Woodland Park.

The ever-increasing financial burden it placed on citizens, who had to pay for the projects, contributed to the Commission's decline after 1830 and it was finally dissolved in 1856. In 1870, it was succeeded by the highly successful Council of Public Works, which planned the next and greatest phase of city expansion.

The park contains several sights and museums covered on other pages: the Széchenyi Spa (*see p37*), the Museum of Transport (*see p71*), the Agricultural Museum (*see p73*), the Amusement Park and the Zoo (*see p153*).

Vajdahunyad Vára (Vajdahunyad Castle)

One of the most popular features of the 1896 Millennial Exhibition held in the City Woodland Park was Ignác Alpár's architectural phantasmagoria, originally a temporary structure, but by popular demand it was subsequently rebuilt in stone (1904–8). It presented a stylistic cross-section of architecture in Hungary through the ages. The Romanesque is represented by a replica of its best-preserved example, the cathedral at Ják in western Hungary, and the baroque by the somewhat heavy neobaroque of the Agricultural Museum. The *pièce de résistance*, however, is Vajdahunyad Castle, which gave its name to the whole complex (its famous original was the seat of the Hunyadi clan in Transylvania). Additional Gothic and Renaissance sections copied from other buildings create a bizarre Hollywood effect, so that you half expect Errol Flynn to jump out of a castle window. In the courtyard is Miklós Ligeti's (*see p94*) fine statue of Béla III's chronicler. The castle replica itself is one-third of the size of the original in Romania.

Városliget is reached by metro to Hősök tere or Széchenyi fürdő.

Vajdahunyad Castle

Városliget

Views of the city

One of the joys of Budapest is that it can be viewed from so many different vantage points. Summer or winter, wind, rain, snow or sunshine, all create different moods and stress different aspects of the city.

Budapest environs

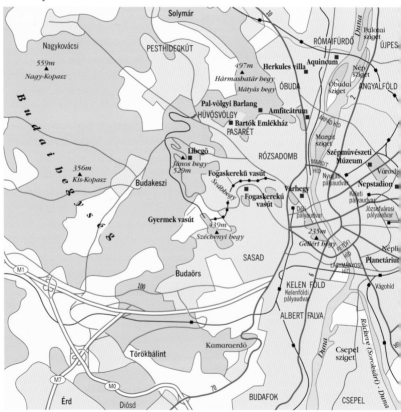

VIEWS FROM BUDA
Budai hegység (Buda Hills)

Just beyond Rózsadomb (Hill of Roses) is the lookout tower on József hegy, with one of the best upstream views of the Danube (take bus 191 from Nyugati pályaudvar to the end stop – Sarolta útca). The Árpád torony on Látó hegy (bus 11 from Batthyány tér to end stop) is a lovely spot.

The highest Buda hill, János hegy (529m/1,736ft), can be reached by bus 21 from Moszkva tér metro; from the end of the line walk through the forest.

(You can also take the chairlift from Zugliget, terminal of bus 158 from Moszkva tér.) On the summit is the celebrated Erzsébet torony tower (1910), named after Queen Elizabeth.

Gellért hegy (Gellért Hill)

For dramatic views over the city and Danube, the best vantage points are from Gellért Hill.
Bus: 27 from Móricz Zsigmond körter, Villányi útca to the stop Búsuló Juhász, then a 400m (440yd) walk.

Várhegy (Castle Hill)

Castle Hill is ringed by bastions. Those on the northern and western sides have been turned into pleasant promenades. Views of the Vérmező (*see p59*) and the residential quarter, Krisztinaváros, can be enjoyed from Tóth Árpád sétány.

On the other side of the hill you can see the Parliament from Fishermen's Bastion (*see p107*). Further along are excellent views from the terraces in front of the Castle Theatre and National Gallery.
Castle Hill districts can be reached by the várbusz from Moszkva tér or bus 16 from Deák Ferenc tér.

VIEWS FROM PEST

Duna korzó (between Chain Bridge and Elizabeth Bridge) offers the best views of the Royal Castle and Castle Hill. For a vista of Pest from an unusual angle, climb the cupola of St Stephen's Basilica (*see pp56–7*) – but be warned: there are over 300 steps!

A city and its river

The Danube is the second-longest river in Europe after the Volga: the Széchenyi lánchíd (Chain Bridge) in Budapest is not yet halfway along its 2,820km (1,752-mile) course. On the Budapest stretch it is generally around 5m (16ft) deep, although there are some holes near Szabadság híd where it plunges to 8 or 9m (26–30ft). The bed is pebbles, loam and sand with outcrops of rock. The flood period is in June, and lowest water levels are reached in October and December.

In Roman times the river was the furthest boundary of the empire and, with its chain of fortresses (*limes*), a formidable barrier to threatening tribes from the east. Thereafter, its greatest value was as a trade route – the 'dustless highway' in a chronicler's picturesque phrase. Goods had to be dragged upstream with teams of horses – or convicts where the bank was too treacherous for animals.

Things changed when the first steamship arrived in 1818. The journey from Pest to Vienna was cut from a month to three days and Hungarian agricultural exports boomed. The importance of Pest as a port was underlined by the scale of Miklós Ybl's imposing Customs House (1874 – now the University of Economics). In the 20th century, a free port was built on the edge of Csepel Island.

Until regulation in the 1870s, floods were a recurring hazard (there were 12 major ones between 1732 and 1838). To improve matters, the main channel was made deeper and narrower, and land was drained along the banks. Both the Parliament and the Technical University were built on reclaimed land. Floods are unlikely to occur nowadays, but, to make sure they don't, ice-breakers are deployed in winter. The bigger problem now is low water, which sometimes forces suspension of shipping.

During World War II all Budapest's bridges were destroyed, making ferries indispensable to cross-river traffic. Only two ferries operate today, in the northeastern part of the city, for use only by people, not vehicles. The Danube is now crossed by ten bridges (two railway and eight pedestrian). The red metro line also crosses it between Parliament and the Batthyány tér.

Today's Danube is a largely tamed creature, the haunt of scullers and canoeists, and a few optimistic anglers on the lookout for some of the 51 species of fish reputed to reside in its grey (seldom blue) waters. Still, the river is the artery of Hungary, inextricably bound up with the nation's history. (*See pp40–41.*)

The mighty Danube

Excursions

At approximately 268km (167 miles) by 528km (328 miles), Hungary is small enough to make most regions accessible from Budapest. Whether you opt for the charms of Lake Balaton or the Hungarian Plain, there will be many sights to keep you occupied.

LAKE BALATON

One hundred kilometres (62 miles) southwest of Budapest is Lake Balaton, Central Europe's largest inland sea. Its warm waters (30°C/86°F in summer) make it Hungary's most popular resort. Sailing, windsurfing and horse riding are additional attractions, as is fishing: there are 40 different species of fish in the lake, the most famous being the indigenous *fogas* (pike-perch).

The delightful country house of Keszthely

Tihany

The Benedictine abbey of Tihany was founded by Andrew I in 1055 and its baroque church contains beautiful carvings by Sebestyén Stulhoff. The ample-bosomed angel on the Altar of the Virgin Mary is supposed to be a portrait of the artist's beloved, a local fisherman's daughter. The Romanesque crypt contains the simple gravestone of King Andrew, who died in 1060.

Other sights of interest include the Abbey Museum. The display covers local topography and the origins of the

Magyars; one room is devoted to the physicist Lóránd Eötvös (1849–1919), who conducted experiments on the Balaton ice-sheet. The rustically furnished House of the Fishermen's Guild, off Pinsky Promenade, has material on the life of the Balaton fishermen. To the north is the Visszhangdomb (Echo Hill), and beyond that the Óvar (old earthern castle ruin). In its rock base Orthodox monks carved out their hermit cells. *www.tihany.hu*

Badacsony

A little further west is the table-top
volcanic mountain of Badacsony. Its
vine-clad slopes produce some of the
region's best wines, notably *Szürkebarát*
(Pinot Gris) of the Pauline monks. The
southeastern face has impressive basalt
columns over 50m (164ft) high. In the
town centre, just north of the main
road, is the József Egry Memorial
Museum, devoted to the Balaton's
famous local painters.

Vines at Badacsony

Keszthely

At the lake's western end is the town of
Keszthely where Count György Festetics
(1755–1819) lived in 'retirement'
(semi-exile) after taking part in a failed
rebellion against the Habsburgs. While
here, he founded the Helikon circle of
reform-minded intellectuals and an
agricultural university known as the
Georgikon. The high point of the tour
of the country mansion is the Helikon
Library, beautifully constructed from
Slavonian oak by a local carpenter. In
the town, the Balaton Museum covers
zoological, ethnological and
archaeological aspects of the region.
www.keszthely.hu

Other places of interest

At the lake's east end the spa of
Balatonfüred has charm. Hévíz (8km/
5 miles) from Keszthely) is a thermal
lake fed by a source 1km (⅔ mile)
below the surface (*the baths are open
8.30am–5pm in summer, 9am–4pm in
winter; www.heviz.hu; frequent buses
from Keszthely railway station to Hévíz*).
The marshy Kis-Balaton at the lake's
western tip, where the River Zala runs
into it, is good for birdwatchers. Along
the southern shore there are many
resorts, of which Siófok is the biggest
and most popular.

The 5km (3-mile) long Csodabogyo's
Cave near Balatonederics is open for
2- and 4-hour tours.
*Tel: (36)20 454 7034;
www.csodabogyos.hu*

Balaton Museum *Múzeum útca 2, Keszthely.
Tel: (06 83) 312 351. Open: Tue–Sun
10am–6pm (Nov–Apr, Tue–Sat 9am–5pm).
Admission charge.*
Festetics Country Mansion *Kastély útca 1,
Keszthely. Tel: (06 83) 312 191. Open: Tue–Sun
10am–5pm; July & Aug, daily 9am–6pm.
Admission charge.*
József Egry Memorial Museum *Egry sétány
12, Badacsony. Tel: (06 87) 431 044;
www.vmmuzeum.hu. Open: May–Sept,
Tue–Sun 10am–6pm.*
Tihany Abbey Museum *1 Andras tér 1
Tel: (06 87) 538 200. Open: May–Sept,
Tue–Sun 9am–6pm; Nov–Mar 10am–4pm; Apr
& Oct 10am–5pm.*

The best way to reach Lake Balaton is by intercity trains, which require reservation (well in advance in summer). See the Thomas Cook European Timetable for times (see pp178–9). Trains leave from Déli pályaudvar (Southern Railway Station) or Keleti pályaudvar (Eastern Railway Station). For bus timetables see www.balatonvolan.hu or www.menetrendek.hu. For more information see www.balaton-tourism.hu

DUNAKANYAR (The Danube Bend)

The Danube enters Hungary flowing west to east, but after Esztergom it is forced into an S-shape in a narrow valley between the Pilis and Börzsöny Mountains. After Visegrád it completes a final loop, thereafter settling on a north–south course. This whole stretch of the river – from Esztergom to Szentendre Island – is known as the Danube Bend, an area of enchantingly dramatic scenery.

Esztergom

Esztergom is where King Stephen was born (c. 975) and where he was crowned on Christmas Day, 1000. He founded Esztergom's archbishopric the following year; Hungarian primates were based here until the Turkish conquest and returned only in the 19th century.
Esztergom is 64km (40 miles) from Budapest on Road 11. Half-hourly buses from Árpád híd (Pest side). Trains from Nyugati pályaudvar. A boat leaves at 8am daily in summer (weekends in low season) from Vigadó tér, Budapest (www.mahartpassnave.hu).

The Basilica

Hungary's largest church, begun in 1822 and completed in 1869, is more imposing than pleasing, but do not miss the red marble funerary chapel (1507) of Archbishop Tamás Bakócz, a relic of the original cathedral. The crypt contains some fine Renaissance sarcophagi and the *kincstár* (treasury) has exquisite gold- and silversmiths' work.
Szent István tér 1. Tel: (06 33) 411 895; www.bazilika-esztergom.hu. Open: Oct–Feb, Tue–Sun 7am–5pm; Mar–Sept, daily 7am–6pm. Free admission. Treasury tel: (06 33) 402 354. Open: Mar–Oct daily 9am–5pm; Nov–Dec 11am–4pm. Closed: Jan & Feb. Admission charge.

Keresztény Múzeum (Christian Museum)

This is in the Víziváros (Water Town). Its greatest treasure is the Lord's Coffin of Garamszentbenedek (c. 1480), which was paraded in Easter processions carrying the figure of Christ crucified.
Mindszenty tér 2. Tel: (06 33) 413 880; www.keresztenymuzeum.hu. Open: Mar–Oct 10am–6pm; Nov & Dec 11am–3pm. Closed: Mon, Jan & Feb. Admission charge.

Vármúzeum (Medieval Royal Castle)

The old castle is just to the south of the basilica. It includes a 12th-century chapel with a fine rose window, the

Hall of Virtues and the room where Stephen was born.
Szent István tér 1. Tel: (06 33) 415 986. Open: Tue–Sun 10am–6pm (until 4pm in winter). Free admission.

Visegrád

The smallest town in the country (population 1,700), *www.visegrad.hu*

Királyi palota (Royal Palace)

Charles Robert of Anjou put Visegrád on the map by building a palace here in 1316. Enlarged and embellished by Sigismund of Luxembourg and Matthias Corvinus in the 15th century, it was rediscovered in the 1930s. You will notice Matthias's coat of arms on the Herkules Fountain. The Lion Fountain (a replica) is so called because sleeping lions support the five columns of the baldachino.
Fő útca 23. Tel: (06 26) 398 026. Open: Tue–Sun 9am–4.30pm. Free admission.

Solomon torony (Solomon's Tower)

The tower was built two centuries after Salomon, son of Andrew I, was imprisoned in Visegrád, so the name is a romantic invention. It houses a museum with remnants from the royal palace.
Mátyás Király Múzeum (King Matthias Museum), tel: (06 26) 398 026; www.visegradmuzeum.hu. Open: May–Oct, Tue–Sun 9am–5pm. Free admission.

It is well worth climbing to the **Fellegvár** (*Citadel, open daily 10am–6pm, to 4pm in winter; tel: (06 26) 398 101*). Admission charge on the path from Nagy Lajos útca. Taxis are available in summer, and from April to September there is a direct bus from Árpád híd terminus. The Hungarian crown jewels were once kept in this powerful fortress on a 350m (1,148ft) high peak. The views over the river and of the Börszöny Mountains are superb.

Visegrád is 40km (25 miles) from Budapest and reached by hourly buses from Árpád híd (Pest side), or via Road 11 by car. Boats run from Vigadó tér twice daily in summer (www.mahartpassnave.hu).

Excursions

The Danube at Visegrád

KECSKEMÉT AND THE ALFÖLD (HUNGARIAN PLAIN)

Kecskemét

Kecskemét flourished as part of the Sultan's personal possessions during the Turkish occupation. In the 19th century its vines were the only ones in Hungary to escape the phylloxera plague, and the town's wealth is reflected in its architecture. The birthplace of the composer Zoltán Kodály and the father of Hungarian drama József Katona, it is also the production centre of the celebrated *barackpálinka* (apricot schnapps).

The main sights are clustered around three central squares. Where Rákóczi útca enters Szabadság tér, on the left is Géza Márkus's Cifra palota (Ornate Palace, 1902), a dazzling Jugendstil building. Opposite it is the Moorish-looking former synagogue (1862), converted in 1966 into a 'House of Science and Culture'. The Town Hall, designed by Ödön Lechner and Gyula Pártos, should not be missed. Its carillon of 37 bells plays at 12.05pm, 6.05pm and 8.05pm.

Kecskemét is 85km (53 miles) south of Budapest and reachable by train (from Nyugati pályaudvar) and bus (from Népliget terminal). By car take M5 and the motorway (toll road – vignette necessary) or the old Road 5. www.kecskemet.hu

The Alföld

Commonly referred to as the *puszta* (abandoned), the once-forested Great Plain was heavily depopulated under the Turks and during the 18th century.

Puszta traditions may be savoured at **Lajosmizse** and **Bugac** where the *csikósok* (cowboys) give displays of

Hungary

horsemanship. At Bugac there is a
Pásztor Múzeum (*open: May–Oct
10am–5pm daily; www.knp.hu*) and a
famous country inn (*csárda*).

At Lajosmizse there is a **Farmhouse
Museum** (Tanyamúzeum). *Tel: (06 76)
356 166. Open: May–Oct Tue–Sun
10am–5pm; closed: Nov–Apr.*

Lajosmizse is to the north on the old Road 5.
Shows 12.30pm daily in summer. **Bugac** is
south of Kecskemét – turn left at
Kiskúnfélegyháza. For tours, contact **Program
Centrum** (*tel: (06 1) 317 7767*) and **Cityrama**
(*tel: (06 1) 302 4382*).

Pécs

The attractive city of Pécs was founded by the Celts, and subsequently (as Sopianae) became the capital of the Roman province of Pannonia Valeria. The early Christian cemeteries here are on the UNESCO World Heritage list. King Stephen established a bishopric here in 1009. Under the Turkish occupation, Pécs was a centre of Islamic culture, boasting five *madrassas* (seminaries) and 17 mosques. In the 18th century, viticulture thrived and coal deposits were discovered, then in the 19th century the city boomed as a result of leather-making and other industries. Uranium deposits were discovered close by in the 1950s.

Remains of the early Christian church in Pécs

The cathedral

The huge neo-Romanesque cathedral above Szent István tér was given its present form by the Viennese architect Friedrich Schmidt between 1882 and 1891, but there are 11th-, 12th- and 14th-century remnants. Inside are 19th-century frescoes by Bertalan Székely, Károly Lotz and others. In the Corpus Christi Chapel look for the Pastoforium of Bishop Szatmáry, a lovely Renaissance altar (1521) in red marble.

Roman remains

Pécs has some of the earliest Christian sanctuaries in Hungary. The Roman tombs at Apáca útca 9 and the remains of the *cella trichora* (clover-leaf chapel) on the opposite side of the street are not always accessible; but the mausoleum (AD 350), just to the north on Szent István tér, is open. It contains frescoes of the Fall and Daniel in the Lion's Den.

Turkish remains

Hungary's best-preserved Turkish monuments are at Pécs. The most impressive is the Mosque of Gazi Kasim Pasha, built in 1579, using the stones of an earlier Christian church. To the west of the town centre is the Mosque of Jakovali Hassan Pasha with a finely carved *minbar* (pulpit). At Nyár útca 8, also to the west, is a *türbe* (sepulchral chapel, 1591). Nearby is the only surviving Turkish fountain.

The cathedral at Pécs

Other sights

The Bishop's Palace, on Dóm tér, is fronted by a modern statue of Franz Liszt. From the other side of the square you enter Káptalan útca through an archway. The street contains no fewer than five museums, of which the Zsolnay Museum (ceramics) is the most interesting. The others – except the one featuring 20th-century Hungarian art – are devoted to individual artists. Walk along Kossuth Lajos útca to see the restored Jugendstil Hotel Palatinus and the neo-rococo theatre, home to Péc's Ballet. In Jókai útca is a splendid Zsolnay well, whose lion's-head spout is copied from the so-called Treasure of Attila discovered in Romania (now in Vienna). The works of Tivadar Csontváry Kosztka (1853–1919), in the Csontváry Museum, express a mystical vision of self and nation. Don't miss his great *Baalbeck* canvas and the poignant *Lonely Cedar*.

Pécs is 180km (112 miles) south of Budapest. See www.pecs.hu.
Direct trains run from Budapest's Déli or Keleti pályaudvar. Buses leave from the terminal beside the Népliget metro.

Csontváry Museum
Janus Pannonius útca 11–13. Tel: (06 72) 310 544. Open: Tue–Sun 10am–6pm.
Mausoleum
Szent István tér. Tel: (06 72) 312 719. Open: Apr–Oct 10am–6pm; Nov–Mar 10am–4pm.
Mosque of Gazi Kasim Pasha
Széchenyi tér, now a Catholic church. Open: summer Mon–Sat 10am–4pm, Sun 11.30am–4pm; winter Mon–Sat 11am–noon, Sun 11.30am–2pm.
Mosque of Jakovali Hassan Pasha
Rákóczi útca 2. Open: Apr–Sept 10am–6pm.
Tomb of Idris Baba
Nyár útca 8. Closed to visitors.
Zsolnay Museum
Káptalan útca 2. Tel: (06 72) 324 822. Open: Tue–Sun 10am–6pm.
Admission charge to all sights.

Blagoveštenska templom

Szentendre

Szentendre (St Andrew) has a Balkan charm rarely encountered in Hungary. It was founded as a town for Serbian refugees after the catastrophic defeat of Serbia by the Turks at Kosovo in 1389. A second wave of immigrants came in 1690, fleeing the wrath of the Turks after an abortive uprising. Both the earlier Hungarian kings and the Habsburgs favoured these refugees from the south. The settlers were able to exploit their trading privileges and the town's proximity to the Danube to become wealthy. Several Orthodox churches were built here in the 18th century, usually on the site of wooden predecessors, each representing a community drawn from a common provenance in the Slav homeland.

The Serb population dwindled during the 20th century and now only about 100 are left out of Szentendre's 20,000 inhabitants. Some of the churches have been sold and are difficult to access.

Szentendre's other claim to fame is the artists' colony started here in the early years of the 20th century and still going strong.
www.szentendre.hu

Belgrád székesegyház (Belgrade Cathedral)

The episcopal church is open only at times of Mass (*Sun 10am, 4pm, Sat 5pm in winter, 6pm in summer*). The iconostasis (1777), the bishop's throne and the pulpit are notable. Do not miss the nearby Szerb Egyházművészeti

Gyűjtemény (Collection of
Ecclesiastical Treasures) which contains
fine icons and other works by
Orthodox masters.
*Pátriárka útca 5. Tel: (06 26) 312 399.
Open: Mar–Sept Tue–Sun 10am–6pm;
Oct–Dec Tue–Sun 10am–4pm; Jan &
Feb Fri–Sun 10am–4pm. Admission
charge.*

Blagoveštenska templom
(Church of the Annunciation)
Commissioned by Greek merchants
and built by Andreas Mayerhoffer
(1754), this church has a fine
iconostasis (1804) by a Serb artist
from Buda.
*Edge of Fő tér. Open: most days
9am–5pm. Admission charge.*

Ferenczy Károly Múzeum
(Károly Ferenczy Museum)
The museum is devoted to artistic
works by the Ferenczy family, of
whom the father, Károly (1862–1917),
was the leading figure in the Nagybánya
artists' colony.
*Fő tér 6. Tel: (06 26) 310 244.
Open: mid-Mar–Sept Tue–Sun
9am–5pm. Admission charge.*

Kovács Margit Múzeum
(Margit Kovács Museum)
Billed as Hungary's leading ceramicist,
Margit Kovács (1902–77) drew on the
traditions of folk art and fine art. The
claims made for her work have been
recklessly inflated.
Vastagh György útca 1. Tel: (06 26) 310

*244. Open: mid-Mar–Sept Tue–Sun
9am–5pm.
Admission charge.*

Marcipán Múzeum
(Marzipan Museum)
*Fő tér 2–4, entrance through the cake
shop. Tel: (06 20) 452 3875;
www.szabomarcipan.hu. Open: daily
10am–6pm.*

Plébániatemplom
(Parish Church of St John)
Steps lead up from Fő tér to Templom
tér, on which stands the church of
the Catholic Dalmatian community.
You can only view it from the porch,
but it is worth the climb for the
marvellous panorama of the town
from the square.

Pozarevacka Church (Church of
St Michael the Archangel)
The church was built in 1763 on the
site of a wooden predecessor. Here and
in the Blagoveštenska an atmospheric
tape of Orthodox chant is played for
the benefit of visitors.
*Kossuth Lajos útca. Open: in summer,
Fri–Sun 11am–5pm. Admission charge.*

Szabadtéri Néprajzi Múzeum
(Village Museum or *Skanzen*)
Known as a *skanzen* after a pioneering
Swedish ethnographical reconstruction
of village life, the museum shows
typical peasant dwellings, churches and
functional agricultural buildings from
ten regions of Hungary. At weekends

there are often demonstrations and folklore programmes.

4km (2 ¹/₂ miles) west of Szentendre on Szabadságforrás útca. Tel: (06 26) 502 500; www.sznm.hu. Open: Apr–Oct Tue– Sun 9am–5pm (until 4pm in winter). Hourly buses from HÉV station. Admission charge, but free on Tue & Wed.

Városi Tömegközlekedési Múzeum (Museum of the Hungarian City Public Transport)

Very interesting for tram fans – near the HÉV terminus (turn right as you exit the HÉV).

Dózsa György útca. Tel: (06 26) 314 280; www.bkv.hu/muzeum/szentendre.html. Open: Apr–Oct Tue–Sun 10am–5pm.

Szentendre is 23km (14 miles) northwest of Budapest. There is a direct rail link (HÉV) from Batthyány tér and hourly buses from Árpád híd bus terminus. Boats leave from Vigadó tér (twice daily in summer, otherwise weekends only; see www.mahartpassnave.hu). Budapest local tickets, passes and the Budapest Card are valid only to Békásmegyer and not to Szentendre on the HÉV. You should buy a supplementary ticket at the station or on the train from the conductor.

Vác

Mentioned by Ptolemy in his *Geographia*, the ancient town of Vác was made an episcopal see by King Stephen. The town was rich – the Vác silver mark was the main local currency of the 14th century – and the bishops

were powerful. One of them, Kristóf Migazzi, had the Triumphal Arch near Március 15 tér erected for Maria Theresa's visit in 1764. Its architect, Isidore Canevale, built the imposing neoclassical cathedral on Konstantin tér in 1777. It contains a fine fresco (*The Trinity* by Franz Anton Maulbertsch) in its cupola.

Worth seeing also are the finds in the crypt of the Dominican church.

34km (21 miles) north of Budapest. Frequent trains from Nyugati pályaudvar. Szentendre and Vác can be seen in one day. Buses run hourly from Szentendre to Váci Rév, where a ferry meets the bus and takes you to the centre of Vác, from where buses return at regular intervals until 10.30pm.

Vácrátót

This fascinating botanical garden comprises 12,000 species of plants and trees, artificial lakes, follies and a watermill.

25km (16 miles) north of Budapest. Hourly trains from Nyugati pályaudvar. By car, take Road 2 to Szödliget and turn right. Alkotmány útca 2–4, tel: (06 28) 369 398. Open: Apr–Oct 8am–6pm; Nov–Mar until 4pm. Admission charge.

Zebegény

Károly Kós's vernacular church is the main sight in this artists' haunt beside the Danube. The stylised frescoes (*Emperor Constantine's Vision of the Cross, St Helena Discovering the True*

Cross) are by the Gödöllő artist Aladár Körösfői-Kriesch (*see p81*).
50km (31 miles) north of Budapest. Roads 2 & 12 via Vác; boats from Vigadó tér (see www.mahartpassnave.hu); the Szob- or Sturovo-bound trains via Vác from Nyugati pályaudvar.

Gödöllő

This baroque mansion is also called the Sissy Mansion after Elizabeth (popularly known as Sissy), wife of the Austro-Hungarian emperor Franz Joseph I (*see p9*) who loved coming here. After 1945 it became a home for aged people and later a Soviet military barracks.
Take the HÉV from Örs Vezér tere until the Szabadság tér stop. Budapest local tickets, passes and the Budapest Card require a supplementary ticket which can be bought at the Örs Vezér tere and Szabadság tér ticket office or on the train

from the conductor. The palace is right across the street. Tel: (06 28) 410 124; www.kiralyikastely.hu. Open: daily 10am–6pm (5pm in winter), last tour at 5pm.

Zsámbék

The ruined Romanesque and late-Gothic church here was built for the Premonstratensians in the 13th century and later taken over by the Paulites. Another attraction here is the Lamp Museum, housed in a typical Swabian cottage (the village was Swabian until the expulsion of many Germans following World War II).
33km (21 miles) west of Budapest. Buses from Széna tér (next to Moszkva tér). www.zsambek.hu. Lamp Museum: Magyar útca 18. Tel: (06 23) 342 212. Open: daily 8am–6pm. Admission charge.

The village of Zsámbék

Getting away from it all

'Budapest and the Danube present one of the most beautiful river-town landscapes anywhere: perhaps the most beautiful in Europe, on a par with London and the Thames or Paris and the Seine.'

JULES ROMAINS
1926

BUDA CAVES

A number of exciting caves have been discovered in the Buda Hills, and four of them can be visited without difficulty. Comprising ancient and long inactive vents for hot springs, the caves have been formed along tectonic fractures.

Castle Hill Caves

The interior of Castle Hill is honeycombed with caves which were structurally improved by the inhabitants over the years. Remnants of Palaeolithic culture have been found here. The 10km (6 miles) of passages and chambers were used in World War II as an air-raid shelter and field hospital. A gruesome waxworks exhibition (Budavári Panoptikum) illustrating the bloodiest scenes of Hungarian history now occupies a part of them.
Úri útca 9. Tel: (06 1) 212 0207.
Open: daily 9.30am–7.30pm.
Admission charge. Bus: 16 or várbusz to Dísz tér.

Gellért hegy Cave (Rock Chapel)

The earliest human habitation of the region was probably in the Gellért caves. A chapel consecrated here in 1926 was walled up by the Communists but reopened in 1990.

Rock Chapel in the caves in Gellért Hill

Szent Gellért rakpart 1. Open: 9am–8pm. Trams: 18, 19, 41, 47, 48 & 49. Bus: 86 to Szent Gellért tér.

Pálvölgyi Barlang

This 7km (4-mile) long cave came to light in 1902 when the son of the local quarry manager squeezed himself through a gap in the rocks. The highlight of the tour is the 'zoo', so called because the drip formations recall elephants and crocodiles.

Szépvölgyi útca 162. Tel: (06 1) 325 9505. Open: Apr–Oct Tue–Sat 10am–4pm. Admission charge. Bus: 65 (five stops) from Kolosy tér, Óbuda.

Szemlőhegyi Barlang

This is renowned for its 'peastone' formations, like bunches of grapes with little stalactites suspended from them. Part of the cave is used for treating people with respiratory diseases. There is a small exhibition about local speleology in the reception building.

Pusztaszeri útca 35. Tel: (06 1) 325 6001. Open: Wed–Mon 10am–4pm. Admission charge. Bus: 29 (four stops) from Kolosy tér, Óbuda.

BUDAI HEGYSÉG (THE BUDA HILLS)

The easiest way of seeing the Buda Hills is to make a tour with the cogwheel railway and the Children's (formerly 'Pioneer') Railway (*see p152*).

The cogwheel railway (Fogaskerekű Vasút) ascends from Városmajor along wooded slopes past the Svábhegy (a Swabian village founded under Maria Theresa), and the Pető Institute for helping brain-damaged children, to Rege útca on Széchenyi-hegy. Nearby is the end-station for the Children's Railway (Gyermekvasút), staffed by children under the supervision of adults. You can take it to the terminus at Hűvösvölgy, or get off at Normafa (first stop) or János hegy (fourth stop) for rambles with convenient return connections. From Normafa, a 2km (1¼-mile) walk (bear left) brings you to the **Budakeszi Game Park**, with return buses to Moszkva tér. From János hegy (529m/1,736ft, lookout tower), a chairlift descends to Zugligeti útca (bus 158 to Moszkva tér).

For the cogwheel railway take trams 18 & 56 from Moszkva tér along Szilágyi Erzsébet fasor to the stop opposite the Hotel Budapest (second stop). The Children's Railway runs every 45– 60 minutes 9am–6.30pm in summer, 9am–5pm in winter. Budapest local tickets and passes are not valid on the Children's Railway. Budakeszi Game Park open: daily 9am–5pm (direct connection with bus 22 from Moszkva tér to Korányi Sanatorium). The János hegy chairlift operates 9am–5pm or 9.30am–4pm according to season.

At the ticket offices for the Pálvölgyi and Szemlőhegyi caves you can apply to join special tours of several other caves not normally open to the public. Appropriate dress will be provided. It is essential that you are fit and in sound health.

Getting away from it all

DANUBE ISLANDS

Of the islands on the Budapest stretch of the Danube, the small Óbuda Island is largely of historical interest: a shipyard was founded here in 1836 on the initiative of Count Széchenyi and worked until the 1990s. At the north end are the ruins of the Roman governor's palace. Margaret Island is the city's loveliest park (*see p58 for details, and pp44–5 for a walk around it*). Csepel Island begins in Budapest and extends to the Great Hungarian Plain.

Csepel sziget (Csepel Island)

This elongated sliver of land begins as Budapest's industrialised 21st District and ends 54km (34 miles) to the south. The origins of the district's heavy industry go back to 1882 when Manfred Weiss founded a factory producing ration tins for troops of the Austro-Hungarian army. He moved to Csepel in 1890 and expanded into armaments. The Communists nationalised the business after the war, and the workers of 'Red Csepel' were supposed to be a bulwark of proletarian solidarity (they even had the dubious pleasure of being represented by the Stalinist dictator Rákosi). Nevertheless, they were the last to hold out against Russian tanks in the 1956 revolution.

Csepel's industry is now largely obsolete and it is planned to use some of its vacant plots for exhibitions and the like. Across the Danube on the Buda side can be seen the restored baroque

PRINCE EUGENE OF SAVOY

The greatest general in the history of Central Europe, Prince Eugene was responsible for clearing Hungary of the Turks after participating in the reconquest of Buda (1686). The Battle of Zenta (1697) was decisive in removing the Ottoman menace once and for all. Eugene was no less successful when allied with the Duke of Marlborough against the French in the War of the Spanish Succession (1701–14). His statue stands before the National Gallery on Castle Hill.

Nagytétényi Castle which has a good display of the history of European furniture. (*Tel: (06 1) 207 0005; www.nagytetenyi.hu. The permament exhibition is free, but there is an admission charge for the temporary exhibitions. Open: Tue–Sun 10am–6pm; bus: 3 from Móricz Zsigmond körtér, from Csepel, bus 138 to Campona shopping mall, and then bus 3 to the Petőti Sándor útca stop.*)

You can see Nagytétényi Kastélymúzeum, Tropicarium and Szoborpark in a day or half day, because the black number 3 bus stops by the Campona mall (where the Tropicarium is) on the way to Nagytétényi. From the Campona, bus 50 goes to the Szoborpark (Statue Park).

Ráckeve

The place most worth visiting on Csepel Island lies to the south, where the ugly industrial suburbs give way to cottages and gardens. Rác means Serb in Hungarian, and the small town was originally populated by Serbs from

Keve, who fled here in the 15th century. Today, of Ráckeve's 8,500 inhabitants, only a handful are Serb.

Szerb templom (Serbian Church)
Ráckeve's church survives and is well worth a visit. The main Gothic structure dates to 1487, but the two side chapels were added later, together with a baroque spire. Inside are colourful frescoes (1771) in Byzantine style by Tódor Gruntovic (who was apparently an Albanian from Kosovo). The sequence begins to the right of the entrance with the Nativity and continues round the church walls, ending with the Resurrection. The baroque iconostasis (1768) is also striking.
Viola útca 1. Tel: (06 24) 485 985; www.tourinform.rackeve.hu. Open: Tue–Sat 10am–noon, 2–5pm, Sun 2–5pm.

The Szerb templom, Ráckeve

Balconies and gabled houses in the Wekerle Settlement

Savoyai Kastély
(Mansion of Prince Eugene of Savoy)

The land on which this delightfully elegant mansion was built originally belonged to the Habsburgs and was sold by them to Prince Eugene after the Turkish wars. He employed Johann Lukas von Hildebrandt (later to build the magnificent Belvedere Palace in Vienna for him) to construct a baroque *Schloss* between 1702 and 1722. The neoclassical dome was added in the 19th century. The splendid interiors have unfortunately been destroyed and the mansion is now a smart hotel. *Kossuth Lajos útca 95. Tel: (06 24) 485 253.*

Ráckeve is 46km (29 miles) south of Budapest. The HÉV suburban train leaves Közvágóhíd terminus in Pest and takes 70 minutes. Trams 2 & 24 end at Közvágóhíd.

Wekerle Telep (Wekerle Settlement)

In the 19th District (Kispest) a remarkable experiment in 20th-century social housing reflects the ambitious plans for city expansion developed by Budapest's mayor István Bárczy.

Inspired by the principles of the English garden suburb, the Wekerle Housing Estate was built over 20 years from 1909 as a completely self-contained village for employees of the municipality. It consists of 650 single-storey villas and 270 bungalows, and bears the name of Sándor Wekerle, the far-sighted and liberal prime minister between 1892 and 1895, and again between 1906 and 1910.

Wekerle reformed the Hungarian currency and successfully fought to limit clerical influence in matters of the state. The principal architect for the estate was the polymath Károly Kós (*see box*), who

KÁROLY KÓS (1883–1977)

Born in Temesvár (now Romanian Timisoara) in Transylvania, Kós won major commissions in Budapest when still in his twenties. As an architect he was influenced by Finnish architecture and the English Arts and Crafts Movement. He was also a gifted writer, illustrating and printing his own works. In Budapest, in addition to the Wekerle Settlement, he designed the buildings for the zoo in 'national romantic style'; dwelling houses that recall the work of Arts and Crafts architect Charles Voysey in England; and schools and churches in the vernacular style.

invested the wooden, gabled and balconied houses with a Transylvanian charm (albeit pseudo). Four ornamental gates stand at the entrances to the central Kós Károly tér. The west gate is particularly interesting, consisting of a huge planked gable rising over rusticated plinths. Another gate mixes vernacular decoration with Renaissance features.

The houses have their own vegetable gardens – a rarity within the city – and the different quarters are divided by leafy avenues and squares. *Metro (blue line) to Határ út; then bus 194 to Kós Károly tér, or bus 99 from Blaha Lujza tér metro, Népszínház útca, via Hatar út metro to Kós Károly tér.*

Getting away from it all

Hungarian folk arts

Hungary's folk traditions have long reflected diverse ethnic groups (Ruthenians, Slavonians, Slovaks, Romanians and Serbs, as well as Magyars). Despite commercialisation, beautiful handicrafts are still produced, and the charm of folk song and dance is undimmed. Surviving peasant homes provide a fascinating insight into a way of life not totally extinct.

Folk art shops are found at all popular tourist spots. Visitors to Budapest may first glimpse folk embroidery as they pass the Transylvanian women who sell their wares at the entrance to the metro or on Castle Hill. Their speciality is the lovely red (or sometimes blue) tulip or heart pattern on a white background. Other regions produce delicate open work, wool-embroidered cushion

Hungarian folk culture includes music, dancing, pottery and textiles

ends, and beautifully ornamented aprons, tablecloths or handkerchiefs. Dense, multicoloured needlework for folk costumes is a Matyó speciality from northern Hungary.

Pottery is a traditional wedding gift. From the Great Plain come water jars with an ochre glaze and attractive coloured pitchers, or plates with flower, bird or star patterns. Look out, too, for the smoky black pottery of Nádudvar in the Hajdúság region.

The horsemen, shepherds and swineherds of the Great Plain specialise in carved artefacts such as whip handles, crooks, axes, mirror frames or tobacco boxes. Look out for beautiful folk carving if you visit the Protestant churches of Southern Transdanubia and the Upper Tisza.

The place to see rural architecture is a *skanzen* (an open-air museum village such as the one at Szentendre, *see p129*).

The houses often had wattle-and-daub walls and roofs thatched with reeds.

Folk entertainment – dancing, singing and seasonal celebrations – may be seen all over Hungary, but especially at Hollókő in the north,

home of the Palóc people. Easter time here harks back to pagan purification and fertility rites. The girls paint beautiful floral designs on eggs, and must run the gauntlet of young men sprinkling them with well water.

A colourful brochure of folklore events and performances is obtainable from Tourinform, *Sütő útca 2, or Liszt Ferenc tér 11. Tel: 800 36 000 000 (toll free) or (361) 438 8080. (Also see Shopping p140.)*

Shopping

In the celebrated Váci útca in the heart of Pest (see p102) you will find long-established shops selling folk art and books alongside newcomers like Adidas. Souvenir-hunters will find plenty to interest them on Castle Hill, while the Fortuna Passage opposite the Hilton has a good bookshop and antiques. Other items to look out for are Herend porcelain and Zsolnay faience. Food delicacies include salami, goose liver and Tokaji wine.

Card use and acceptance is increasing. Most big shops and petrol stations accept Visa, Visa Electron Eurocard/MasterCard and Maestro cards. American Express and Diners Club are less used by Hungarians.

Antiques

The state-owned chain **Bizományi Áruház Vállalat (BÁV)** is best for antiques and furniture.
Szent István körút 3. Tel: (06 1) 473 0666. Ferenciek tere 10. Tel: (06 1) 318 3733. Kossuth Lajos útca 1 and 3. Tel: (06 1) 317 3718 and (06 1) 318 8608. Branches near Ferenciek tere.

Patina
Váci útca 46. Tel: (06 1) 337 9627.

Régiség-Vári Antikvitás
Szentháromság útca 7 (Castle Hill). Tel: (06 1) 212 3715.

Art galleries

BÁV Galéria
Falk Miksa útca 21. Tel: (06 1) 353 1975.

Dorottya Galéria
Dorottya útca 8. Tel: (06 1) 266 0877.

Kogart-Ház
Andrássy útca 112. Tel: (06 1) 354 3820; www.kogart.hu

Books and maps

There are many secondhand bookshops on the Múzeum körút. Other good shops to visit:

Cartographia
The largest selection of maps is available here.
Bajcsy-Zsilinszky útca 37. Tel: (06 1) 312 6001.

Központi Antikvárium
Old prints; also second-hand books.
Múzeum körút 13–15. Tel: (06 1) 317 3781.

Térképkirály (Mapking)
The biggest map shop in Hungary.
Szugló útca 83–85. www.mapking.hu. Open: Mon–Fri 8am–6pm, Sat 8am–1pm. Tram: 3, 62; bus: 32 to Szugló útca.

Children's wear

Bambini
Margit körút 56. Anker köz 1. Villányi útca 42.

Brendon
Váci útca 168. Tel: (06 1) 329 9704; www.brendon.hu

Delicatessens

La Boutique des Vins
The owner is chef of the Gundel Restaurant.

József Attila útca 12.
Tel: (06 1) 317 5919.
PICK
The house of the famous
Hungarian salami.
Near the Parliament,
Kossuth Lajos tér 9.
Tel: (06 1) 331 7783.
T Nagy Tamás Cheeses
Gerlóczy útca 3.
Tel: (06 1) 317 4268.

Department stores
Corvin
Blaha Lujza tér 1.
Tel: (06 1) 266 7788.

Folk art
Embroidery, lace, faience,
wax figures and painted
Easter eggs.
Folkart Centrum
Váci útca 58.
Tel: (06 1) 318 5840;
www.folkartcentrum.hu.
Open: daily 10am–7pm.
Hungaricum Shop
Fortuna útca 18.
Tel: (06 1) 487 7306.
Open: daily 9am–9pm.

Foreign-language bookshops
Alexandra (Duna Plaza)
Váci útca 178.
Tel: (06 1) 238 0594.
Bestsellers
English and American
books and newspapers.

Október 6 útca 11.
Tel: (06 1) 312 1295;
www.bestsellers.hu
Litea Bookshop and
Tea-Garden
Hess András tér 4
(Fortuna Passage).
Tel: (06 1) 375 6987.

Music
Rózsavölgyi
Zeneműbolt
Szervita tér 5.
Tel: (06 1) 318 3500;
www.rozsavolgyi.hu

Shoes
Vass Handmade Shoes
Haris köz 2.
Tel: (06 1) 318 2375.

MALLS
Budapest now also has
numerous new shopping
centres (malls). Every
mall has a supermarket,
restaurants and toilets.
   Mall shops also open
10am–8pm, Mon–Sat,
and until 6pm on Sun.
Arena Plaza
Newest and largest mall
being constructed now.
Kerepesi útca. Metro:
Stadionok.
Árkád
Örs Vezér tere 25.
Tel: (06 1) 433 1414.
Metro: Örs Vezér tere.

Campona
Has a tropicarium, an
oceanarium and indoor
rainforest.
Nagytétényi útca 37–45.
Tel: (06 1) 424 3000;
www.campona.hu.
Tétény-busz fast bus from
Szent Gellért tér Mon–Fri,
or bus 3 daily from
Móricz Zsigmond Körtér.
Duna Plaza
Váci útca 178.
Tel: (06 1) 465 1666;
www.dunaplaza.net.
Metro and bus 4 to
Gyöngyösi útca.
Europark
Üllői útca 201.
Tel: (06 1) 347 1607;
www.europark.hu.
Metro: Határ útca.
Mammut I and II
Houses a multiplex
cinema, bowling alley
and 300 shops.
Széna tér. Tel: (06 1) 345
8020; www.mammut.hu.
Trams: 4 & 6 to Széna tér;
metro: Moszkva tér.
Westend City Center
400 shops, a roof garden
and cinema.
Váci útca 1–3. Tel: (06 1)
238 7777; www.westend.
hu. Tram: 4, 6; bus: 6,
26, 91, 191; metro:
Nyugati pályaudvar.

Shopping

MARKETS
Flea markets

The legendary flea markets (*bolhapiac*) of Budapest, though not for the faint-hearted, are a paradise for junk fanatics. Since the collapse of Communism the amount of Marxist-Leninist bric-à-brac to be found in them has increased; there are even Russian army uniforms and caps, sold off by impoverished Soviet troops before their departure.

Ecseri Piac (Ecseri Flea Market)

This was officially renamed Használtcikk (used items) market after one of its several moves from its original location on Ecseri útca, but everyone uses the old name. The outer stalls (*kirakodó*) are loaded with knicknacks – most of them uninspiring, the good stuff having been sold to dealers in the early hours. These dealers (many of them Slavs or gypsies) occupy booths in the centre, and it is here that you might find bargains. Much of their stock comes from peasants, persuaded to part with their family heirlooms when the dealers canvassed a village.

The most interesting goods at Ecseri are decorative silver and Russian icons. Unfortunately, the silver is usually being sold illegally (under Hungarian law a permit is required to deal in it), while the icons may well have been looted from Ukrainian churches. Not long ago the police confiscated some icons that had been stolen from somewhere near Chernobyl – on the grounds that they were contaminated with radiation, not because they were

Vegetables on display

stolen! Other items of interest said to crop up include bentwood chairs made by the Viennese Thonet company, old radios and copper lamps. It is best to go to Ecseri with a Hungarian who knows the ropes and you should beware of pickpockets.

Nagykőrösi útca 156 in the 19th District. Open: Mon–Fri 8am–4pm, Sat 8am–3pm. Bus 54 from Boráros tér to the Fiume útca stop, or bus 154 Mon–Fri from Határ útca metro station to the Használt Cikk Piac stop.

Józsefvárosi Piac
(Market in the Józsefváros)

The self-styled Worldwide Business Centre is really a Third World souk. Traders come from as far afield as China and Vietnam, but chiefly from the former Soviet Union, Bulgaria and Romania. They trade cheap goods for things not available back home. American kitsch is big here, as is liquor of uncertain provenance, used car parts, cigarette lighters – anything, in short, that might have fallen off the back of a lorry or turned up in the attic.

Kőbányai útca 9 (10th District). Open: daily until 1pm. Tram: 28 from Blaha Lujza tér; bus: 9 from Deák Ferenc tér.

Another interesting flea market is held outside the **Petőfi Hall** (Petőfi Csarnok) in the Városliget.

www.bolhapiac.com. Open: Sat & Sun 7am–2pm. Metro: Széchenyi fürdő; trolleybus: 70, 72, 74.

Food and general markets
Központi Vásárcsarnok
(Central Market)

This is a fabulous 19th-century covered market. It was one of five opened in the 1890s (*see p30*) and is a protected monument. There are over 100 stalls on two floors selling meat, vegetables, fruit, and even flower seeds and pottery; note that most stalls close around noon.

Vámház körút 1–3. Tel: (06 1) 217 6865. Open: Mon–Thur 6am–4pm, Fri 6am–7pm, Sat 6am–3pm. Tram: 47, 49; bus: 15, citybusz; trolleybus: 83 to Fővám tér.

Lehel Piac (Lehel Market)

Futuristic market hall opened in 2002 in an old market location.

Metro: Lehel tér.

Rákóczi Téri Csarnok
(Market Hall on Rákóczi tér)

Another market hall from the 1890s.

Rákóczi tér 7–8. Tel: (06 1) 210 2565. Tram: 4, 6.

Western supermarkets have moved in on Budapest – including Spar and Tesco. Every shopping mall also has a supermarket, usually a Spar or Match. Tesco is open 24 hours daily except public holidays. The two stores most convenient for tourists are Fogarasi útca (trolleybus 80 to Pillangó útca from the Keleti pályaudvar, or walk from Pillangó útca metro) and Váci útca (bus 4 from Deák Ferenc tér to Tesco); *www.tesco.hu*

Entertainment

Entertainment in Hungary covers everything from traditional folk music and festivals to more highbrow events such as the ballet, opera and classical music concerts. Cinema is a long-standing art form in this part of the world too, and both home-grown and mainstream American films can be seen.

Ballet

Ballet is not a major feature of the Budapest scene, but performances by prima ballerinas Katalin Volf and Ildikó Pongor are worth looking out for. The *corps de ballet* is resident at the State Opera. Foreign companies make guest appearances at Budapest arts festivals (*see p147*). Ballets and musicals are usually staged in the **Thália Theatre** (Thália Szihaz)
Nagymezö útca 22–24. Tel: (06 1) 312 4230; www.thalia.hu.

Cinema

The cinematic tradition is strong in Hungary and there are currently over 20 cinemas in Budapest. Works by directors such as Miklós Jancsó, Pál Sándor and István Szabó will be well known to Western film buffs. Although the big co-productions such as *Colonel Redl* or *Mephisto* have been widely exposed abroad, the occasional Budapest summer season of home-grown movies affords a chance to see more obscure works with English subtitles. *Pesti Műsor* is the best source for information on such events – look under *A budapesti mozik műsora* (you'll need a friend on hand to translate). *Pest Est*, a cinema programme (*www.pestiest.hu*), is available free at cinemas, bars and restaurants, though it is in Hungarian.

Films in English, German, French and Italian

You can see most recent mainstream films with the original soundtrack at the multiplexes in the numerous shopping centres (*see p141*). The best sources of information are the detailed movie programmes in *Budapest Week* (*www.budapestweek.hu*) and *The Budapest Sun* (*www.budapestsun.com*), and also see *www.xpatloop.com*. Classics are shown at the Örökmozgo Filmmúzeum (*Erzsébet Körút 39. Tel: (06 1) 342 2167*). There are usually some seven or eight films in the repertory.

Opera

Opera is popular in Hungary and has a distinguished tradition going back to the opening of Miklós Ybl's opera house in 1882 (*see pp78–9*). New productions are staged during the spring music festival and the autumn/winter season.

If you want Hungarian opera, look for Bartók's *Kékszakállú herceg vára* (Bluebeard's Castle), Erkel's *Bánk Bán*, Goldmark's *Sába királynöje* (The Queen of Sheba) and Kódaly's *Háry János*.

The State Opera went through a bad patch in the last phase of Communism because of incompetent management; the main problem today is lack of money. However, leading expatriate singers (Sylvia Sass or Éva Marton, for instance) sometimes visit.

Opera venues

**Magyar Állami Operaház
(State Opera House)**
*Andrássy útca 22. Tel: (06 1) 353 0170.
Box office at Andrássy útca 20.
Tel: (06 1) 332 7914; www.opera hu*
Erkel Színház (Erkel Theatre)
Köztársaság tér 30. Tel: (06 1) 333 0540.

Operetta and musicals

The heyday of operetta (*see pp84–5*) followed the formation of the Austro-Hungarian Empire in 1867 and lasted until the end of World War I. It has been largely superseded by the musical, of which two popular Hungarian examples are the rock-operas *István, a király* (*Stephen the King*) and *Attila.*

Operetta venues

**Fővárosi Operett Színház
(Operetta Theatre)**
*Nagymezo útca 17. Tel: (06 1) 353 2172;
www.operettszinhhaz.hu*
Pesti Vigadó (The Pest Redoute)
The theatre offered a programme but remains closed for renovation until 2009.
*Vigadó tér 2. Tel: (06 1) 354 3755;
www.vigado.hu*

Theatre

The obvious problem about visiting the theatre in Budapest is the language barrier. **Katona József Theatre** (Petőfi Sándor útca 6, *tel: (06 1) 318 6599;
www.szinhaz.hu*) provides English-language summaries of plays on request. **Merlin Theatre** (Gerlóczy útca 4, *tel: (06 1) 317 9338;
www.merlinszinhaz.hu*) is currently the only venue for English-language productions. The latest on the city scene is the **Hungarian National Theatre** (Nemzeti Színház).
*Bajor Gizi park 1. Tel: (06 1) 476 6800;
www.nemzetiszinhaz.hu.
Tram: 2, 24 to Vágóhíd útca.*

Ballet performances are well attended

MUSIC

In Hungary the classical tradition, nutured by the Music Academy (*see pp80–81 & 83*), is very strong. Names such as Széll, Solti, Doráti and Ormándy are familiar to all music lovers.

The new generation includes outstanding soloists such as Dezsö Ránki and Zoltán Kocsis (piano), Vilmos Szabadi (violin) and Miklós Perényi (cello). Distinguished composers of the past such as Franz Liszt, Ferenc Erkel, Béla Bartók, Zoltán Kodály, Ernö Dohnány, as well as individuals such as György Ligeti and György Kurtág, have left their mark on the modern music scene.

BOOKING FOR MUSICAL PERFORMANCES

Tickets for classical music (symphony concerts, chamber music and recitals) are sold at the Központi Jegyirodá (Central Booking Office) at Andrássy útca 15 (*tel: (06 1) 267 1267*). Tickets for outdoor performances in summer are sold at: Ticket Express, Andrássy útca 18 (*tel: (06 30) 303 0999; www. ticketexpress.hu and www.tex.hu*). Otherwise apply to the box offices at the venues concerned.

Pesti Műsor publishes information on forthcoming musical events every Thursday under 'zene' in the English-language newspapers and in brochures obtainable from Tourinform (*see p188*).

The Central Ticket Office carries the useful Koncert Kalendárium published in both Hungarian and German, listing musical events a month in advance.

Main classical music venues

**Budapest Kongresszusi Központ
(Budapest Convention Centre)**
A large modern concert hall away from the centre.
Jagelló útca 1–3. Tel: (06 1) 372 5700.

**Pesti Vigadó
(The Pest Redoute)**
(*See pp79–80 & 145.*)
*Vigadó tér 2. Tel: (06 1) 354 3755;
www.vigado.hu*

**Zeneakadémia
(Music Academy)**
Highly recommended for acoustics and exotic architecture.
*Liszt Ferenc tér 8. Tel: (06 1) 342 0179;
www.zeneakademia.hu*

The new **Müvészetek Palotája
(Palace of Arts)** houses the Nemzeti Hangversenterem (National Concert Hall), and opened in 2005.
*Bajor Gizi park 1. Tel: (06 1) 555 3000;
www.mupa.hu. Tram: 2, 24 to
Vágóhíd útca.*

Frequent organ and choral music performances are also held in the Matthias Church and St Stephen's Basilica.

Modern music

If you prefer New Wave, visit
TRAFO (*Liliom útca 41. Tel: (06 1)
215 1600; www.trafo.hu*), or
Petőfi Csarnok, venue for many famous concerts (*Zichy Mihály útca 14.
Tel: (36 1) 251 7266;
www.petoficsarnok.hu*).

Folk music

**Fövárosi Müvelödési Ház
(City Cultural House)**

Easily the best group for Hungarian folk music (Muzsikás with Márta Sebestyén) plays here on Tuesdays from 5pm.
*Fehérvári útca 47.
Tel: (06 1) 203 3868.*

**Hagyományok Háza
(House of the Traditions)**

Home of the State Folk Ensemble.
Corvin tér 8. Tel: (06 1) 201 5928.

Festivals

The first important music month of the year is March, with the Budapest Spring Festival during its second half. The festival offers '10 days of 1,000 events in 100 venues', and many big-name musicians make guest appearances. Festival programmes can be obtained from Tourinform, *tel: (06 1) 486 3311*, or *www.festivalcity.hu*

Summer sees performances on the open-air stages of the city (notably opera at the Margaret Island Theatre, *tel: (06 1) 340 5540*) and at venues within striking distance of the capital (for example, at the country house at Martonvásár). Baroque operas are now being performed each summer in the courtyard of the Zichy Palace in Óbuda. There is an autumn Festival of Church Music, which provides a good chance to hear interesting works by Hungarian composers past and present. In November, a choral festival entitled *Vox*

Traditional zither player

Pacis takes place. The number of events and mini-festivals is continually increasing with sponsorship.

The fledgling Budapest Fringe comes to town in April (*www.budapestfringe.com*).

The week-long Sziget Festival (*www.sziget.hu*) held on Óbudai Island (*sziget*) in midsummer is fast becoming one of the hottest european festivals. Join thousands of others for days of eclectic music.

In July it hosts the risqué Lesbian, Gay, Bisexual and Transgender Festival (*www.budapestpride.hu*).
HÉV: from Batthyány tér metro to Fiatorigát.

The Roma and their music

The Roma first came to Hungary in the 15th century from Asia through the Balkan region, and are now the largest minority in the country (five per cent of the population); they are also the most underprivileged. In the public mind they are associated less with music than with poverty, crime and unemployment. Though no longer nomadic, they are still among the most deprived section of society. To combat this, a Roma Parliament was recently formed, and its leaders are trying to raise national consciousness and improve their tainted image.

Music has traditionally offered a way out of the cultural ghetto. Musicians accompanied conscription drives across the land in the 18th century; Roma bands played for the nobility and the gentry in the 19th century, when they began to become figures of romance. Around the turn of the century they were romanticised in operettas like *Gypsy Life* (1904),

Traditional Roma musicians

A Roma festival with dancing

Gypsy Love (1910) and *Gypsy Bandleader* (1912) (gypsy, however, has become a derogatory word today). In the late 19th century, the Neue Freie Presse in Vienna pointed out how members of Roma musician families had benefited from the Hungarian Roma cult: 'They no longer tell fortunes or ply the tinker's trade, but instead put on a dinner jacket and fiddle for the *beau monde* from eleven at night till five in the morning.'

Contrary to popular belief, what the musicians play is not the true music of the Roma. According to the composer Béla Bartók, 'They are simply performers of Hungarian popular song'; and he added: 'There is of course gypsy music – songs with texts in gypsy language. These are never played or sung by gypsies in public.'

Today the smarter restaurants in Budapest all have their own Roma ensemble playing evergreens from Viennese operetta and the frenzied Hungarian *csárdás*. These are the aristocrats of their world, famous for their ready wit and happy-go-lucky temperament, unextinguished by centuries of persecution.

The 'Ybl Kiosk', now a casino

NIGHTLIFE

Budapest's nightlife has shed any residual prudery and embraced the hedonistic lifestyle with many bars and clubs open until dawn, and super-clubs cropping up with winter and outdoor summer venues. Stag weekenders have arrived along with the budget airlines, too. The following venues are some of the best in the city and usually incorporate a restaurant and DJ. For listings, check *www.pestiside.hu* and *www.funzine.hu*

Casinos

Tropicana Casino
Vidagó útca 2.
Tel: (06 1) 266 3062;
www.tropicanacasino.hu.
Open: 2pm–5am.

Várkert Casino
Sophisticated casino in the former 'Ybl Kiosk' (Royal Castle pumphouse).
Ybl Miklós tér 9.
Tel: (06 1) 202 4244;
www.varkert.com.
Open: 2pm–5am.

Bars/clubs

A38 Hajó
Pázmány Péter sétány.
Tel: (06 1) 464 3940;

www.a38.hu. Open:
4pm–4am (restaurant:
11am–midnight). Tram:
4, 6 to Petőfi híd.

**Bahnhof Music Club
and Bank Dance Hall**
*Teréz körút 55, behind
the Nyugati Railway
Station. Bahnhof
tel: (06 1) 302 4751;
Bank Dance Hall
tel: (06 20) 344 4888;
www.bankdancehall.hu*

Bed
Reményi Ede útca 3.
Tel: (06 70) 208 8389;
www.bed.hu

**Buddha Beach/
Retro Beach**
Közraktár útca 9–11.
www.beachside.hu.
Open: Mon–Fri noon–5am;
Sat & Sun 3pm–5am.
Tram: 2 to Zsil útca.

Dokk
*Lövőház útca 2–6
(Mammut 2).*
Tel: (06 1) 436 3666;
www.dokkcafe.hu.
Metro: Moszkva tér.

Irish Cat Pub
Múzeum körút 41.
Tel: (06 1) 266 4085;
www.irishcat.hu.
Open: daily 11am–2am.
Metro: Kálvin tér.

Piaf
Nagymező útca 25.
Tel: (06 1) 312 3823.

Open: 10pm–7am.
Metro: Opera.
Szoda
Wesselényi útca 18.
Tel: (06 1) 461 007;
www.szoda.com.
Open: Mon–Fri 9am–6am;
Sat & Sun 2pm–6am.
Metro: Astoria.

Jazz
Cotton Club
The famous songs of the
1920s and 30s.
Jókai útca 26.
Tel: (06 1) 354 0886;
www.cottonclub.hu.
Open: noon–1am.
Jazz Garden
Authentic modern and
swing.
Veres Pálné útca 44/A.
Tel: (06 1) 266 7364.
Open: daily 6pm–2am;
www.jazzgarden.hu

One unique aspect of Budapest is its courtyard venues: loud,
basic and brilliant, the art is graffiti, the glasses are plastic and
the kitchen is open late. Try one of the following locations:
Szimpla Kert
Kazinczy útca 14; www.szimpla.hu.
Open: daily noon–2am. Metro: Astoria.
West Balkán
Futó útca 46. Tel: (06 20) 473 3651.
Open: daily 9am–6am. Metro or trams: 4, 6 to Ferenc körút.
Zöld Pardon
Summer-long (Apr–Sept) outdoor festival with swimming
pool, food and music.
Goldmann Gyögy tér; www.zp.hu.
Open: daily 9am–6am. Tram: 4, 6 to Petöfi híd.

Live music
Kodor Klub
Erzsébet tér. Tel: (06 20)
201 3868;
www.godorklub.hu.
Open: daily 9am–1am.
Metro: Deák Ferenc tér.
Morrisons Pub
Révay útca 25. Tel: (06 1)
269 4060; www.morrisons.
hu. Open: daily 6pm–
6am. Metro: Kálvin tér.

Old Man's Pub
Akácfa útca 13.
Tel: (06 1) 322 7645;
www.oldmans.hu.
Open: daily 3pm–4am.
Metro: Blaha Lujza tér.
Rolling Rock Café
Bartók Béla útca 76.
Tel: (06 1) 385 3348;
www.caferollingrock.hu.
Open: daily 11am–2am.

A typical floor show, Pest-style

Children

The suggestions below are for activities largely unaffected by the language barrier. Parents could also consider a visit to a stalactite cave or the Buda Hills (see p133) or, in summer, a boat trip on the Danube.

Bábszinház (Puppet Show)

Shows are based mainly on international and Hungarian fairy tales. *Andrássy útca 69. Tel: (06 1) 321 5200. Ticket office open: daily 9am–6pm. Metro: Vörösmarty útca.*

Csodák Palotája (Palace of Miracles)

Central Europe's first interactive scientific playhouse. *Millenáris park. Tel: (06 1) 350 6131; www.csodakpalotaja.hu. Open: Mon–Fri 9am–5pm, Sat & Sun 10am–6pm. Tram: 4 & 6 to Széna tér; metro: Moszkva tér.*

Gellért Gyógyfürdő (Gellért Baths)

There are many baths (*see pp36–7*) but Gellért offers the bubble bath inside and the wave bath outside.

Gyermekvasút (Children's Railway)

Formerly the 'Pioneer Railway' of the Communist youth movement, running 11km (7 miles) between Széchenyi-hegy and Hűvösvölgy. The driver is adult but the staff are children. (*See also p133.*) *www.gyermekvasut.com. Széchenyi-hegy is reached by the Fogaskerekű Vasút (cogwheel railway), whose terminus is opposite Hotel Budapest, Szilágyi Erzsébet fasor 47; tram: 18, 56, 118. The Hüvösvölgy terminus is by the last stop of tram 56.*

Kölyökpark (Kidpark)

Indoor play for children under 12. *Lövőhaz útca 1–5 (Mammut 2). Tel: (06 1) 345 8512; www.kolyokpark.hu. Open: daily 10am–8pm.*

Margit sziget (Margaret Island)

Bicycles can be hired at the southern end. At the northern end is the Japanese Garden and a 'singing well' that plays a tune every hour. (*See pp44–5.*)

Museums

Bélyegmúzeum (Stamp Museum)
Eleven million stamps!

Hársfa útca 47. Tel: (06 1) 341 5526;
www.belyegmuzeum.hu. Open: Tue–Sun
10am–6pm (until 4pm Nov–Mar).
Admission charge. Trolleybus: 74.

Füsti Magyar Vasúttörténti park
(Hungarian Railway History Park)
Over a hundred railway vehicles.
Tatai útca 95. Tel: (06 1) 238 0558;
www.lokopark.hu. Open: Apr–Oct
Tue–Sun 10am–6pm; Nov, Dec & Mar
Tue–Sun 10am–3pm. Closed: Jan & Feb.
Bus: 30 from Keleti pályaudvar to the
Rokolya útca stop, special trains from the
Nyugati railway station. The Nostalgie
Train is free with a pre-purchased park
entrance ticket, which is obtainable in
the Mávnosztalgia shop at platform 10
of the Nyugati station. The trains run
Apr–Oct.

Postsai és Távközlési Múzeum
(Post Museum)
Models, coaches and a message
despatch tube to play with.
Andrássy útca 3. Tel: (06 1) 269 6838;
www.postamuzeum.hu. Open: Tue–Sun
10am–6pm (until 4pm Nov–Mar).
Admission charge. Metro: Bajcsy-
Zsilinszky útca.

Telefónia Múzeum
(Telephone Museum)
Úri útca 49. Tel: (06 1) 201 8188;
www.postamuzeum.hu. Open: Tue–Sun
10am–4pm. Admission charge. Várbusz
to Szentháromság tér.
See also Museums pp70–77.

Planetárium
Laser and special shows for children.
Népliget. Tel: (06 1) 265 0725;

www.planetarium.hu and for the Laser
Theatre www.lezerszinhaz.hu.
Admission charge. Metro: Népliget.

Tropicarium
Largest aquarium in Central Europe.
Nagytétényi útca 37–45. Tel: (06 1) 424
3053; www.tropicarium.hu. Open: daily
10am–8pm. Tétény-busz fast bus line
from Szent Gellért tér Mon–Fri, or black
No 3 from Móricz Zsigmond körtér, daily
to the Lépcsős útca stop.

Városliget (City Woodland Park)
Állatkert (Zoo)
Three thousand animals.
Állatkerti körút 6–12. Tel: (06 1) 273
4900; www.zoobudapest.com. Open:
9am–6pm, until 5pm Mar, Apr, Sept &
Oct and until 7pm on summer weekends
(4pm in winter). Admission charge.

Fövárosi Nagycirkusz (Circus)
Állatkerti körút 7. Tel: (06 1) 343 8300;
www.maciva.hu. Shows: Wed–Fri 3pm or
5pm; Sat also at 10.30am & 7pm; Sun
also at 10.30am. Ticket office open: daily
10am–6pm.

Vidám Park (Amusement Park)
Talk is that the park will close – call for
information.
Állatkerti körút 14–16. Tel: (06 1) 363
8310; www.vidampark.hu. Open:
May–Aug 10am–8pm, mid-Mar–Apr,
Sept & Oct 10am–6pm or 7pm
depending on the day. Closed: Nov–Feb.

Trolleybus 72 from the metro stop at
Arany János útca or metro to Széchenyi
fürdő brings you close to all of the above .

Sport and leisure

Magyars are great football fans and Hungary has produced some charismatic players such as Ferenc Puskás. They also excel in sports such as swimming and water polo, no doubt helped by the top-class training facilities available.

SPECTATOR SPORTS
Cycle racing
There is a championship track with a capacity of 14,000 for enthusiasts.
Millenáris Cycle Track, Stefánia útca 2. Tel: (06 1) 471 4100. Bus: 7.

Football
International matches are held in the Puskás Ferenc Stadion (former Népstadion) (*Istvánmezei út 3–7, tel: (06 1) 471 4100; metro: Stadionok*), which holds 76,000 spectators. The two leading Budapest teams are Ferencvárosi Torna Club (FTC), whose ground is at Üllői útca 129 (*tel: (06 1) 215 6025; metro: Népliget*), and Kispest-Honvéd (*Új temető útca 1–3; tel: (06 1) 282 9789; tram 42 from the metro stop at Határ út*). Matches are played at weekends and on Wednesday evenings. Information from the monthly *Programme* obtainable at Tourinform, *Sütő útca 2.*

Horse racing
Flat racing (*galopp*) and trotting races (*ügető*) take place at Kincsem Park, Albertirsai útca 2 (*tel: (06 1) 263 7818; metro to Pillangó útca or Expó-Bus and Kingcem Park – bus on race days from Örs Vezér tere metro to Expótér*); see *www.magyarturf.hu* for racing days. Punters may place bets at the tote.

Hungarian Grand Prix
The Grand Prix is held annually in early August at the Mogyoród circuit, 24km (15 miles) northeast of Budapest (reached by car on the M3 motorway; bus terminus varies yearly); or HÉV from Örs Vezér tere metro towards Gödöllő or Mogyoród to the temporary Hungaroring stop and walk.

SPORTS FACILITIES
Aerobics
Andrea Mozgás Stúdió
Hold útca 29. Tel: (06 1) 311 0740.
Astoria Fitness Centre
Károly körút 4. Tel: (06 1) 317 0452.

Bowling

Strike Bowling Club
Budafoki útca 111–113.
Tel: (06 1) 206 2754.
Mammut Bowling Centre
Mammut Shopping Mall.
Tel: (06 1) 345 8300.
Westend Bowling Club
Westend City Centre by the Nyugati
pályaudvar. Tel: (06 1) 238 7040.

Cycling

Hungarian roads are dangerous, but
cycle paths are being created.
Tourinform should have a map of routes
(*Budapest Kerék-párútjai*). Bicycle shops
include Bike Cserny Shop and Service
(*Zuhatag sor 12, tel: (061) 200 6837*) and
Rokon Bicycle (*III District Mátyás Király*
útca 6, tel: (06 1) 250 3038).

Fishing

Not allowed between 20 April and
20 May. Contact MOHOSZ (Hungarian
Fishing Association, *Korompai útca 17;*
tel: (06 1) 248 2590; www.mohosz.hu)
for information and permits.

Golf

Golf Tanya
Obudai (Hajógyári) Sziget 410.
Tel: (06 1) 437 9038; www.golftanya.hu;
email: golftanya@golftanya.hu or see
www.golfcourses.hu for other golf clubs.

Horse riding

Budapesti Lovas Klub
Huge hall for winter exercise.
Kerepesi útca 7. Tel: (06 1) 313 5210.

Petneházy Country Club
Riding in the hills. Lessons for all levels.
Feketefej útca 2–4. Tel: (06 1) 391 8010.

Running

The Budapest Marathon is held yearly
(see *www.budapestmarathon.com*).

Squash

Top Squash Club
Also has a sauna and bowling.
Széna tér. Tel: (06 1) 345 8193.

Swimming

Sports pools include:
Hajós Alfréd Nemzeti Sportuszoda
(Alfréd Hajós Sport Pool)
Margit Sziget. Tel: (06 1) 340 4946.
Open: Mon–Fri 6am–5pm, weekends
6am–6pm. Bus: 26 from Nyugati
pályaudvar or Árpád híd metro.
Nyéki Imre Uszoda
(Imre Nyéki Swimming Pool)
Large 33m (108ft), 8-lane pool.
Kondorosi útca 14. Tel: (06 1) 208 4025.
Open: Mon–Fri 6am–6.30pm, weekends
6am–7.30pm. Tram: 18, 41, 47, 118 to
Albertfalva Kitérő.

Tennis

There are over 30 tennis clubs and hotel
courts. Try:
CEU Conference Center
Kerepesi útca 87. Tel: (06 1) 327 3150.
Flamenco Hotel
Tas vezér útca 7. Tel: (06 1) 889 5600.
Holiday Beach Budapest Wellness &
Conference Hotel
Piroska útca 3–5. Tel: (06 1) 463 7160.

Dog days in Budapest

Non-experts could be forgiven for looking blank at the mention of an *agár*, a *puli*, a *pumi* or a *mudi*. All of them are high-performance canines bred by a people with a passion for working dogs.

The classic Hungarian breeds are believed to have accompanied the seven Magyar tribes across the Carpathians 1,100 years ago. Of these, the shaggy black *puli*, which looks like an animated hearthrug, is something of a national symbol. It is still unrivalled for rounding up sheep at pasture. Something bigger was needed to keep predators at bay, and this task was performed by the bulky *komondors* and *kuvasz* (easily distinguishable from wolves and other marauders by their white colour).

The beautiful *vizsla*, a ginger-coloured retriever, was kept by the

Hungary is truly a nation of dog lovers, as reflected in this street art

Most people own dogs as pets and there are also many breeds of working dogs, such as the *puli* (above right)

Árpád kings as early as the 11th century, and the greyhound-like *agár* (also of Asian origin) was used for deer-hunting by the nobility.

Dog-fanciers can now spot (or buy) Hungarian and other breeds at the twice-yearly dog sale on Marczibányi tér. In the early days of Communism luxury breeds were virtually banned, and vets would only attend working animals. Now, dogs are once again a status symbol – and often a protection against burglars.

The European Dog Show was held in May 1993 in the Sportcsarnok of the Népstadion, proving that Budapest is back on the international canine map. Exhibitors came from 14 countries, including the USA and Russia, to this annual event where the fate of 6,000 glamorous dogs was decided by a panel of international judges. In a world of economic gloom and general disillusionment the dog show arouses enormous enthusiasm; Hungarians, it seems, are happy to share the view of the Marquise de Sévigné, who once observed: 'The more I see of men, the more I admire dogs.'

Food and drink

Restaurants are mushrooming, long-established ones have been given a facelift, and, while foreign investment has affected every area, fast food, beer cellars and the luxury end of the market have benefited especially from new capital.

Types of eating house

There are three main categories of eating house: an *étterem* offers a large selection of dishes and can be any price category; a *vendéglő* should offer something more like home cooking with fewer dishes to choose from, and also tends to have more ambience. *Vendéglő* prices used to be more moderate, but many have been subjected to the same sort of gentrification as similar establishments in other countries, which invariably means higher prices. A *csárda* is a country-style inn with a relatively restricted menu and simple fare. Smaller establishments with cheaper prices are called *bisztró* or, if self-service, *önkiszolgáló* or *ételbár*. A *söröző* is a beer cellar, which usually serves (fairly basic) food.

The better-class restaurants should be booked in advance, at least for an evening. Always ask for a menu showing all the prices before ordering. The vast majority of restaurants in Budapest are legitimate businesses offering good value and service, but overcharging has been known. It occurs almost always on or near the Váci útca.

Hungarian cuisine

Most people's idea of Hungarian cooking begins and ends with goulash, a dish that in Hungary itself bears little resemblance to the anaemic version served elsewhere. We think of it as a stew, but it is just as likely to be encountered as a rich meaty soup (*gulyásleves*). The origins of *gulyáshús* lie in the nomadic period of the Magyars; their horsemen would often travel for days in hostile terrain carrying iron rations of stewed mutton or beef, dried and preserved in a bag made from a sheep's stomach. To prepare a meal they would simply soften the meat in boiling water, creating a sort of instant stew. It is believed that this contributed to the success of their campaigns – the enemy had to waste time killing and cooking their food.

There is a great deal more to Hungarian cuisine than goulash, however. Hungary's geographical position ensured that surrounding cultures had an impact on its cooking: Balkan influence is seen in the stuffed vegetables; the sausage culture has been modified by German and Italian practices; and dumplings were borrowed from the Slavs. The lands of historic Hungary had their own regional dishes, such as tarragon lamb stew from Transylvania and *lecsó* (peppers and tomatoes stewed in lard) from southern Hungary.

The basis of most Hungarian food preparation is a heavy roux of pork lard and flour, known as *rántás*, liberally spiced. Many dishes include sour cream or smoked sausage, thus creating the characteristic combination of astringent and smoky tastes.

Pork (*sertés*) is the most frequent meat on the menu, usually in some kind of *pörkölt* (stew). Beef (*marha*) is

Hungarian wines are made from some of the world's most succulent grapes

not common and is seldom good quality, with one striking exception: Budapestians are fanatic consumers of steak tartare, and many restaurants serve it with all the trappings. Lamb (*bárány*, *birka*) is hard to come by.

Soups (*leves*) play a major role in Hungarian cooking. In summer an excellent cold sour cherry soup (*meggyleves*) is often on offer, while fish restaurants serve a fish soup (*halászlé*), the speciality of Szeged in southern Hungary. Freshwater fish (carp, pike, perch) from the Danube, the Tisza and Lake Balaton can be good, although it is best to order a fillet if you dislike bones. The best fish is *fogas* (pike-perch): the Gundel chef serves it with cream-cheese sauce on a bed of spinach. More mundane are the meat and poultry dishes fried in breadcrumbs (*rántott hús*, *rántott csirke*). Chicken paprika (*paprikás csirke*), prepared with paprika spice and sour cream, provides the tongue-tingling flavours the Magyars love. Vegetables come either stuffed (*töltött*), with cabbage, peppers, etc, or in a *főzelék*, a delicious semi-purée (the marrow one – *tökfőzelék* – is especially good).

The choice of puddings is limited, perhaps because Hungarians are well catered for by pastry shops and cafés; however, pancakes (especially the version stuffed with curds – *túró*) are a nice way to round off a meal. A sponge confection with chocolate sauce and whipped cream (*somlói galuska*) is held in affection by the locals.

Menu reader

GENERAL PHRASES

Étlapot kérnék	I would like the menu
Fizethetek kártyával?	May I pay by credit card?
Fizetni szeretnék	I would like to pay
Hozzon kérem ...	bring me ... please

ELŐETELEK (HORS D'OEUVRES)

gombafejek	
rántva	fried mushrooms
hortobágyi	meat pancake with
palacsinta	sour cream
libamáj	goose liver

LEVESEK (SOUPS)

bableves	bean soup
gulyásleves	goulash soup
halászlé	fishermen's broth
meggyleves	sour cherry soup

KÉSZÉTELEK (READY DISHES)

borjú pörkölt	veal stew
sertés pörkölt	pork stew
töltött káposzta	stuffed cabbage
töltött paprika	stuffed pepper

FRISSENSÜLTEK (DISHES PREPARED TO ORDER)

halételek	fish
Balatoni fogas	Balaton pike-perch
csuka	pike
ponty rántva	fried carp
süllő	young pike-perch

HÚSÉTELEK (MEAT)

fatányéros	mixed grill
magyaros tál	fried meat and vegetables
sertésmáj	pig's liver

SZÁRNYASOK (POULTRY)

kacsa	duck
liba	goose
paprikás csirke	paprika chicken

VADAK/ VADMADARAK (GAME)

fácán	pheasant
fogoly	partridge
nyúl	hare
őzhús/szarvashús	venison
vaddisznó	wild boar
vadkacsa	wild duck
vadliba	wild goose

TÉSZTÁK (PASTA/RICE)

galuska	small dumplings
káposztás kocka	pasta with cabbage
rizs	rice
tarhonya	pasta grains
túrós csusza	pasta layers with cottage cheese

GOMBÓCOK (DUMPLINGS)

barackos gombóc	apricot dumpling
szilvás gombóc	plum dumpling

FŐZELÉK	**(VEGETABLES)**
burgonya	potato
hasábburgonya	French fries
főtt krumpli	boiled potatoes
sült krumpli	roast potatoes
fokhagyma	garlic
hagyma	onion
káposzta	cabbage
zöldbabfőzelék	French beans
zöldpaprika	green pepper

SALÁTÁK	**(SALADS)**
fejes saláta	lettuce
káposztasaláta	cabbage salad
paradicsom	tomato
savanyúság	pickles
uborkasaláta	cucumber salad
(vizes) uborka	gherkin

ÉDESSÉGEK	**(DESSERTS)**
fagylalt	ice cream
gesztenye püré	chestnut purée
'Gundel' palacsinta	pancake with chocolate sauce and ground walnuts

GYÜMÖLCSÖK	**(FRUIT)**
alma	apple
banán	banana
citrom	lemon
cseresznye	cherry
meggy	Morello cherry
eper	strawberry
körte	pear
málna	raspberry

narancs	orange
őszibarack	peach
(sárga) barack	apricot
szilva	plum

ITALOK	**(DRINKS)**
fehér bor	white wine
vörös bor	red wine
édes	sweet
száraz	dry
pezsgő	'champagne' (usually Sekt)
likör	liqueur
pálinka	
schnapps	(fruit-based) brandy
csapolt sör	draught beer
dobozos sör	canned beer
üveges sör	bottled beer
üditők	soft drinks
szénsavmentes ásványvíz	still mineral water
szénsavas ásványvíz	sparkling mineral water
szódavíz	soda water
jég	ice
gyümölcslé	fruit juice
kávé	coffee
tea citrommal	tea with lemon
tejes tea	tea with milk

WHERE TO EAT

Prices for all restaurants are quoted in four categories which should be taken as guidelines rather than exact figures. Average meal prices per head are given, excluding drinks and service (customarily 10 per cent). Service is not included unless stated on the menu-card. Inflation in Hungary is around 5 to 9 per cent, so expect price rises.

★ up to 1,000 Ft (fast food, snack bars, etc)

★★ up to 2,000 Ft

★★★ up to 3,000 Ft

★★★★ over 3,000 Ft

Hungarian

Aranyszarvas ★★★★

A famous game restaurant in a neoclassical house in the Tabán. Mouth-watering wild boar stew and pheasant. Reasonably restrained gypsy band.

Szarvas tér 1.
Tel: (06 1) 375 6451;
www.aranyszarvas.hu.
Open: daily noon–11pm.
Bus: 5, 78, 86 to Szarvas tér.

Bagolyvár ★★★

Part of the Gundel empire, but cheaper. It concentrates on a few traditional dishes changed on a daily basis.

Állatkerti útca 2.
Tel: (06 1) 468 3110;
www.bagolyvar.com.
Open: daily noon–11pm.
Metro: Hősök tere.

Csarnok Étterem ★★

A very popular, typical Hungarian eating place with outside seating in summer.

Hold útca 11. Tel: (06 1) 269 4906. Open: 11.30am–10pm. Trolleybus: 70, 78 to Honvéd útca.

Csendes ★★

Friendly service, good value. Transylvanian specialities. Ideal for lunch.

Múzeum körút 13. Tel: (06 1) 267 0218. Open: Mon–Sat noon–10pm. Metro: Astoria.

Dio ★★★★

Modern décor housing Hungarian dishes with modern twists and flavours, and Hungarian wine.

Sas útca 4. Tel: (06 1) 328 0360;
www.diorestaurant.com. Open: daily noon–midnight. Metro: Arany János útca.

Fözelék faló ★

Small, functional and fast… typical Hungarian *fözelék*, a kind of soup with your choice of meat, cheese and veg on top.

Nagymező útca 18. Tel: (06 1) 302 3856. Open: 9am–8pm; Sat 10am–5pm. Closed: Sun. Metro: Opera.

Gundel ★★★★

Hungarian *haute cuisine* in elegant surroundings. The most famous restaurant in Hungary. Reservations essential.

Állatkerti útca 2. Tel: (06 1) 468 4040;
www.gundel.hu. Open: daily noon–3pm, 6.30pm–midnight. Metro: Hősök tere.

Kéhli Vendéglő ★★★

Really excellent Hungarian cooking; aficionados rave about the bone marrow served in a red pot.

Mókus útca 22 (Óbuda). Tel: (06 1) 250 4241;
www.kehli.hu. Open: daily noon–midnight. Near the Aquincum Hotel.

Kék Rózsa ★★

Join the locals at this down-home Hungarian kitchen.

Wesselényi útca 9.
Tel: (06 1) 342 8981; www.
blueroserestaurant.eu.
Open: daily 11am–10pm.
Metro: Astoria.

Kispipa Vendéglő ★★★

Famous for its incredibly long and illegible menu. Interwar ambience, old-fashioned service. Reserve ahead.

Akácfa útca 38. Tel: (06 1)
342 2587. Open: Mon–Sat
noon–1am. Tram: 4, 6 to
Wesselényi útca.

Uj Sipos Halászkert ★★★

If you want to try fishermen's broth (*halászlé*), pike-perch (*fogas*) or carp (*ponty*), this could be the place for you. Balaton white wines to wash it down. Music in the evening Mon–Sat from 7pm.

Fő tér 6 (Óbuda).
Tel: (01) 388 8745;
www.ujsipos.hu.
Tram: 1.

Sir Lancelot ★★★

Medieval dining and ambience.

Podmaniczky útca 14.
Tel: (06 1) 302 4456;
www.sirlancelot.hu. Open:

noon–1am. Trolleybus: 72,
73 to Teréz könít.

Tabáni Kakas
Vendéglő ★★★

The chef stresses that almost all dishes are cooked with goose fat, not lard. The chicken casserole is much praised.

Attila útca 27. Tel: (06 1)
375 7165. Open: daily
noon–10pm. Bus: 5, 78,
86 to Szarvas tér.

Tüköry Söröző ★★

A place for steak tartare buffs. Home cooking, engagingly shabby décor.

Hold útca 15.
Tel: (06 1) 269 5027;
www.tukory.hu.
Open: Mon–Fri
11am–midnight. Metro:
Arany János útca.

Zsákbamacskához ★★★

A mouthful of a name provides traditional home-cooked Hungarian food.

Lovag útca 3.
Tel: (06 1) 354 1810;
www.zsakbamacska.hu.
Open: daily noon–
midnight. Metro:
Nyugati Pályaudvar.

Dried paprika, chillies and garlic

Paprika and *pálinka*

The Hungarian temperament is often said to be ardent and volatile, qualities that are mirrored in the national taste for hot spice (paprika) and fiery spirits (*pálinka*). The most famous of the firewaters is apricot schnapps (*barack-pálinka*), the best of which is distilled on the Alföld (Great Hungarian Plain) at Kecskemét. It is made from two varieties of apricot, the *kajszi* and the more juicy *rakovsky*, which has a strong aroma. The crushed stones of the apricots are added to the juice, and the liquid is fermented in oak barrels for at least a year. The best *barack* is sold in bottles with a white label featuring a picture of the Kecskemét town hall. Some *barack* comes in traditional long-necked flasks known as 'whistlers' (*fütyülős*) or in a *kulacs* made of Herend porcelain. The Hungarian custom is to down your *pálinka* in one gulp, which can be disconcerting, especially as it is usually drunk on an empty stomach as an aperitif.

Paprika, or capsicum, was probably introduced into Hungary in the 16th century by the Bulgarian retainers of the Turks (Bulgarians were traditionally great horticulturists). The poorer classes began using it as a condiment, a habit that spread to the nobility in the 19th century. The great Hungarian biochemist Albert Szent-Györgyi stumbled on capsicum's curative properties by accident, when working at Szeged University. He hated paprika, but his wife was convinced it was good for him and packed some in his luncheon box every day. Unable to eat it, he decided instead to see what it contained; his analysis led him to the discovery of Vitamin C – and a Nobel Prize.

Paprika is grown all over Hungary, but the best is said to come from Szeged and Kalocsa in the south. In this region you can see the decorative strings of paprika pods hung out to dry on the verandas of peasant houses. There are several different types: a small and hot red one, a large sweeter red version, a green one and the succulent yellow, ideal for eating raw with salami. Almost all typically Hungarian soups and main dishes are spiced with paprika.

DISHES WITH PAPRIKA

All kinds of *pörkölt* (stew) (*see p159*)
halászlé (fish soup)
paprikás csirke (paprika chicken)
hortobágyi husos palacsinta
(meat pancake filled with stew)
gulyásleves (goulash soup)
paprikás krumpli (paprika potatoes).

No Hungarian meal is complete without paprika

International/ continental cuisine

Apetito ★★★★

Breakfast, small 'apetitos' and fine dining at the castle with a superb sommelier.

Hess András tér 6.
Tel: (06 1) 488 7416;
www.apetito.hu.
Open: daily
noon–midnight.
Metro: Batthyány tér.

Bel Canto ★★★★

A truly classic restaurant with superb dining, wines and singing staff appropriately adjacent to the Opera.

Dalszínház útca 8.
Tel: (06 1) 269 2786;
www.belcanto.hu.
Open: noon–3pm,
5pm–2am; Sun by
appointment.
Metro: Opera.

Café Kor ★★★

Stunning menu and a superb wine list in a classic yet laid-back dining room.

Sas útca 17.
Tel: (06 1) 311 0053.
Open: daily 10am–10pm.
Metro: Arany János útca.

Callas ★★★★

Divine art nouveau interior with terrace for fine dining, coffee and cocktails.

Andrássy útca 20.
Tel: (06 1) 354 0954.
Open: 8am– midnight;
Fri & Sat 8am–2am.
Metro: Opera.

Robinson ★★★★

Attractively located on a raft on the lake of Városliget (City Woodland Park). Carefully chosen menu of international and Hungarian dishes. Guitar music.

Városligeti tó,
Állatkerti körút 1.
Tel: (06 1) 422 0224;
www.
robinsonrestaurant.hu.
Open: daily noon–4pm,
6pm–midnight (weekends
dinner only).
Metro: Hősök tere.

Vadrózsa ★★★★

The most fashionable restaurant in town, situated in a baroque villa on the Rózsadomb. Extremely expensive set-price meal, no menu and no wine list (the waiter advises). Terrace in summer.

Pentelei Molnár útca 15.
Tel: (06 1) 326 5817.
Open: daily noon–3pm
and 7pm–midnight.
Bus: 91 to Vérhalom tér,
or take a taxi.

American

Iguana Restaurant ★★

Mexican food.

Zoltán útca. Tel: (06 1)
331 4352. Open: daily
11.30am–midnight. Tram:
2, 2A; metro and
trolleybus: 70, 78 to
Kossuth Lajos tér.

Balkan (Serbian)

Szerb Vendéglő ★★

Simple and cheap option for trying Balkan cuisine.

Nacm Ignác útca 16.
Tel: (06 1) 269 3139.
Open: Mon–Sat
11am–11pm, Sun
11am–4pm.
Metro, tram: 4, 6; bus: 6,
26, 91, 191 to Nyugati
pályaudvar or 15, citybusz
to Markó útca.

Czech & Slovak

Szlovák Söröző ★★

Big portions of Slovak specialities, but also Hungarian dishes.

Bihari Fános útca 17.
Tel: (06 1) 269 3108.
Open: 11am–1am; Fri &
Sat 11pm–2am; Sun
11am–midnight.
Metro, tram: 4, 6;
bus: 6, 26, 86, 91, 191 to
Nyugati pályaudvar or 15
to Marko útca.

French

Le Jardin de Paris ★★★★
Bistro-style atmospheric restaurant with French wines on offer – at a price. Late-night opening with live jazz in the evenings.
Fő útca 20. Tel: (06 1) 201 0047. Open: daily noon–midnight. Metro: Batthyány tér.

Fusion

Goa ★★★
Asian fusion plus Italian dishes in Zen surroundings with WiFi. Reservations recommended.
Andrássy útca 8. Tel: (06 1) 302 2570; www.goaworld.hu. Open: daily noon–midnight. Metro: Opera.

Manna ★★★
On Castle Hill, this new location is attracting Budapest's epicureans.
Palota útca 17. Tel: (06 20) 999 9188; www.mannalounge.hu. Open: daily noon– midnight (6pm–1am in winter). Bus: 16.

Mokka ★★★★
Dark wood and leather interior host cocktails and fresh Asian fusion cuisine.

Sas útca 4. Tel: (06 1) 328 0081; www.mokkarestaurant.hu. Open: daily noon– midnight. Metro: Arany János útca.

Spoon Café & Lounge ★★★★
New hot spot in a many-layered, eclectic entertainment venue. Excellent kitchen to match the view.
Vigadó tér 3. Tel: (06 1) 411 09 33; www.spooncafe.hu. Open: 10am–2am.

German

Kaltenberg ★★
Bavarian food in typically massive portions.

Kinizsi útca 30–36. Tel: (06 1) 215 9792. Open: noon–midnight. Metro: Ferenc körút; tram: 4, 6 to Üllői út.

Italian

Il Terzo Cerchio ★★
Superb neighbourhood Italian; all Italian kitchen and staff in the Jewish Quarter.
Dohany útca 40. Tel: (06 1) 354 0788; www.ilterzocerchio.hu. Open: daily noon– midnight. Metro: Astoria.

Trattoria Toscana ★★★
Tuscan specialities and atmosphere.
Belgrád rakpart 13.

Pizzas have arrived in a big way

Beer halls are good value and the choice of foreign beer is increasing all the time

Tel: (06 1) 327 0045;
www.toscana.hu.
Open: noon–midnight
daily. Tram: 2, 2A; bus: 5,
7, 8, 14, 78, 112, 173,
citybusz; metro:
Ferenciek tere.

Japanese
Fuji Japan
Restaurant ★★★★
In a pagoda-like interior
where enthusiasts can
watch the chef at work.
Csatárka útca 54/B.
Tel: (06 1) 325 7111;
www.fujirestaurant.hu.
Open: noon–11pm.
Bus: 11 from Batthyány
tér metro.

Vegetarian
Vegetárium ★★
All there is for
vegetarians in the city,
apart from salad bars.
Has a good reputation
among the cognoscenti.
Cukor útca 3.
Tel: (06 1) 484 0848;
www.vegetarium.hu.
Open: daily noon–10pm.
Metro: Ferenciek tere.

Sörözok (beer halls)
Budapest beer cannot
compare with Czech or
German brews, which
are increasingly available
in the capital. Austrian
beer (particularly the
ubiquitous Gösser) is also
common, due to heavy
Austrian investment in
Hungarian breweries.
Becketts Irish Bar ★★
Authentic Irish pub with
live entertainment.

Bajcsy–Zsilinszky útca 72.
Tel: (06 1) 311 1035;
www.becketts.hu. Open:
noon–1am. Metro:
Nyugati páyaudvar.
Paulaner Bräuhaus
The Bavarian brew plus
accompanying food and
atmosphere.
Alkotás útca 53 (Mom
Park). Tel: (06 1) 224 2020;
www.paulanersorhaz.hu.
Open: daily 11am–1am.
Tram: 63.

Kavezok, Cukraszdak (cafés, cake shops)
Recapture the spirit of
a more leisured age.
Angelika ★
A favourite meeting place
on the Buda side, cosy in
winter, cool in summer
on the terrace.

Batthyány tér 7.
Open: daily 10am–10pm.
Metro: Batthyány tér.

Centrál Kávéház ★★
Restored to its late 19th-century days of glory.
This popular café also serves lunch and dinner.
Károlyi Mihály útca 9.
Tel: (06 1) 266 2110;
www.centralkavehaz.hu.
Open: 8am–midnight.
Bus: 7, 15, 78, 173;
citybusz to Ferenciek tere;
tram: 2, 2A.

Gerbeaud ★★
The most famous of
Pest's cafés since Swiss
patissier Emil Gerbeaud
took it over in 1883.
Period interior, excellent
pastries (which you can
also take away).
Vörösmarty tér 7.
Tel: (06 1) 429 9000;
www.gerbeaud.hu.
Open: daily 9am–9pm.
Metro: Vörösmarty tér.

Gerlóczy Kávéház
Gorgeous café, crêperie
and restaurant on a quiet
square, with WiFi, live
jazz/folk music and a
hotel coming soon.
V Ker Gérlóczy útca 1.
Tel: (06 1) 234 0953;
www.gerloczy.hu. Open:
7am–11pm; Sat & Sun
8am–11pm. Metro:
Deák Ferenc tér.

Lukács ★
Said to have the best
pastries in town. Nostalgic
atmosphere and décor.
Andrássy útca 79.
Tel: (06 1) 302 8747.
Open: daily 9am–8pm.
Metro: Oktogon.

Művész ★
Delightful early 20th-century interior. Usually
full of musicians and
artistes.
Andrássy útca 29.
Tel: (06 1) 352 1337.
Open: daily 9am–
midnight. Metro: Opera.

Ruszwurm ★
A famous and charming
café with original
Biedermeier cherrywood
furnishings. The cream
slice (*krémes*) is the best
in town.
Szentháromság útca 7.
Tel: (06 1) 375 5284.
Open: daily 9am–8pm.
Várbusz: to
Szentháromság tér.

The most famous cake shop in Hungary, Gerbeaud

Wines of Hungary

To wine buffs familiar only with the much-promoted *Egri Bikavér* (Bulls' Blood from Eger), Hungarian viticulture offers the prospect of interesting discoveries. The country has 16 wine-growing regions producing many refreshing and somewhat acidic white wines, together with a number of full-bodied reds. Most Hungarian wine is drunk young, and over-production of poor-quality plonk is endemic, made worse by the collapse of the huge Russian market. (When asked why he did not export the resultant surplus elsewhere, one producer gravely replied: 'Because it is unfit for human consumption.')

To learn about the better-quality wines one could do worse than visit the Magyar Borok Háza (House of Hungarian Wines), where there is a

Hungarian suppliers are now producing top-quality wines

choice of 1,000 wines from all regions and tasting is possible (*Szentháromság tér 6, Castle Hill, tel: (06 1) 212 1031; www.magyarborokhaza.hu; open: daily noon–8pm*).

The best white wines come from the volcanic Badacsony plateau on the northern shore of Lake Balaton, from Gyöngyös in northern Hungary and from the Tokaji Hills, although there is also extensive production on the Great Plain. Native grapes like Hárslevelű (Lime Leaf) or Furmint from Tokaj produce pleasantly drinkable wines, while Szürkebarát (Pinot Gris) and Olaszriszling (Italian Riesling) are good Balaton products. The best reds come from the Villány region of southern Hungary, whose Cabernet Sauvignons and Merlots are occasionally outstanding.

Uniquely Hungarian is the famous golden dessert wine Tokaji Aszú – 'the wine of kings and king of wines'. Once you have tried it you will understand the enthusiasm of Pope Benedict XIV, who wrote to thank Maria Theresa for a consignment in the 18th century and delivered a graceful eulogy of Tokaji: 'Blessed is the land that produced you, blessed the lady who sent you; and blessed am I who drink you.'

Hotels and accommodation

New, historic, design boutique and luxury hotels are continually being built to accommodate Budapest's growing tourist numbers. These must cater for around five million visitors annually. Availability can be strained at peak times (midsummer, when the Grand Prix is held, Christmas and New Year).

Those who can be more flexible than business people in a hurry should have little problem finding accommodation, provided they are happy to consider staying in the private rooms that double the bed supply at peak periods. For hotels it is vital to book in advance from abroad if you want a specific location or facility (for example, a Danube view or a quiet room not overlooking a main thoroughfare).

You should bear in mind that mid-price hotels may have taken block bookings from tour operators up to a year in advance; there remains a shortage of this sort of accommodation because of the obsession of developers with profitable luxury hotels.

Prices

As elsewhere in Eastern Europe the standards prevailing in any given star category may not always match up to the expectations of Western visitors, though this mostly applies to older establishments in the upper mid-price bracket. Even then there may be compensations (for instance, the Gellért's wonderful spa makes up for its less pleasing bedrooms). More recent hotels all meet the highest European standards (the five-star Grand Hotel Corvinus Kempinski, opened in 1992, and the delightful Thermal Aquincum in Old Buda, for example). The long-established waterfront hotels in Pest also maintain a high level of service; one of them, Duna Intercontinental, has been acquired by Marriott Hotels.

The following price structure indicates what one might expect to pay for a double room with breakfast in different categories of accommodation in Budapest. Inflation is running at around 5 to 9 per cent, but the luxury hotels adjust their prices more in line with international norms.

★★★★★ 40,000 Ft or above
★★★★ 20,000 to 40,000 Ft
★★★ 12,000 to 20,000 Ft
★★ 10,000 to 12,000 Ft
Pensions: 8,000 to 20,000 Ft.

The cost of a private room may be cheaper still – it should be possible to find a pleasant room at around 6,000 Ft (probably not including breakfast), and even less in a hostel.

Location

The decision where to stay in the city is likely to be determined by convenience and aesthetics in that order. If you stay in the Buda Hills (for example in the Hotel Agro or Normafa) the air is good, but you have a longish trek into the city. Castle Hill has the best of all worlds – a lovely situation, cleaner air and rapid access to the centre; unfortunately, your choice here is limited to the relatively expensive Hilton and the small Kulturinnov Hotel. There are some cheaper hotels in the Víziváros below Castle Hill on the Buda side.

The distinguished spa hotel the Gellért

On the Pest side there are two hotels with classic waterfront locations (the erstwhile Fórum, now Inter-Continental and the Marriott) and two within spitting distance of the river (Sofitel Atrium and Four Seasons Gresham Palace).

Otherwise, your choice is mostly from hotels in the densely built heart of Pest or along the boulevards. In addition, there are several good hotels beyond or around the Tabán/Gellért Hill area (Mercure Budapest Buda, Victoria, Flamenco and Gellért).

Booking agencies (hotels, private rooms, apartments)

In the high season you may well be greeted at the railway termini and outside booking agencies by private individuals with rooms to let. If you prefer a more formal arrangement, there are various agencies that will help you find the sort of accommodation you require. If you want a private room, look for the desk marked *fizetővendég* (paying guest service). In such accommodation, bathroom and kitchen facilities may have to be shared, and a stay of less than four days attracts a supplement of 30 per cent.

IBUSZ

3,000 rooms available!
Main office: Ferenciek tere 10. Tel: (06 1) 485 2767; fax: (06 1) 337 1205; www.ibusz.hu. Open: Mon–Fri 9am–6pm, Sat 9am–1pm. Closed: Sun. Metro or bus: 7, 15, 78, 173 & citybusz to Ferenciek tere; or tram 2, 2A; bus 5, 8, 15 & citybusz to Március 15 tér.

Non-Stop Hotel Service

Apáczai Csere János útca 1 (behind Hotel Marriott). Tel: (06 1) 266 8042; www.non-stophotelservice.hu. Open: daily 9am–10pm (8pm in winter). Metro: Ferenciek tere; bus: 7, 15, 78, 173, citybusz to Ferenciek tere; bus: 15, citybusz to Petőfi tér; tram: 2, 2A to Vigadó tér.

Hotels

Luxury hotels

The luxurious **Grand Hotel Corvinus Kempinski** (*tel: (06 1) 429 3777*) has been joined by the superb **Boscolo Hotel, The New York Palace** (*tel: (06 1) 886 6111*). Historical luxury at the new **St George Residence** (*tel: (06 1) 393 5700*).

The **Hilton** (*tel: (06 1) 889 6600*) has a superb view and good location in the

Hotel Thermal Aquincum

old town of Buda. The three riverfront hotels – the **Budapest Marriott** (currently being renovated, *tel: (06 1) 266 7000)*, **Inter-Continental** (*tel: (06 1) 327 6333*) and **Sofitel Atrium** (*tel: (06 1) 266 1234*) – and the luxury **Four Seasons Hotel Gresham Palace** (*tel: (06 1) 268 6000*) offer fine views of the Royal Palace and Castle Hill. New, and very central, is the **Le Meridien** (*tel: (06 1) 429 5500*).

Mid-range hotels

The **Mercure** group has refurbished historic locations and now has seven hotels (*tel: (06 1) 485 3100*). The **Ibis** group now has four central hotels providing their cookie-cutter rooms (*tel: (06 1) 456 4100*). The **Novotel Centrum** (*tel: (06 1) 477 5300*) is an art nouveau delight. You'll notice mellow mood hotels all over the city from the luxury **Klotild** (*tel: (06 1) 413 2062*) to the boutique **Cosmo** (*tel: (06 1) 413 7213*) and the ever-popular **Marco Polo Hostel** (*tel: (06 1) 413 2555*). The new boutique hotel **Hotel Zara** (*tel: (06 1) 357 6170*) has made quite an impact.

One place with character is the old **Astoria** (*tel: (06 1) 889 6000*), which has been refurbished but retains its traditional ambience.

Thermal hotels

A speciality of Budapest is the spa hotel, of which the **Gellért** (*tel: (06 1) 889 5500*) is the most distinguished. There are two spa hotels on the lovely Margaret Island: the **Thermal**

(*tel: (06 1) 889 4700*) and the **Grand Hotel** (*tel: (06 1) 889 4700*), the latter in a restored building designed by Miklós Ybl. An attractive addition to the hotel scene is the **Hotel Corinthia Aquincum** in Óbuda (*tel: (06 1) 436 4100*).

Smaller hotels and pensions

If you want a hotel that is different (but very spartan), the **Citadella** (*tel: (06 1) 466 5794*) on the summit of Gellért Hill has 11 rooms, or there's the **Botel Fortuna (Ship-Hotel)** on the Danube at the Szent István Park (*tel: (361) 288 8100*). There are three-star rooms and a youth hostel on board. Many pensions are also quite a long way out, but they are almost always homely and pleasant. Economical and centrally located between the Opera House and Oktogon is **Hotel Medosz** (*tel: (06 1) 353 1700*).

Youth hostels

Book online (*www.gomio.com* or *www.hostelworld.com*) for confirmed reservations – the best hostels are often full – and discounted prices.

Camping

The fairly central and grassy **Haller Camping** (*tel: (06 1) 476 3418*) is good.

On the Internet information is available at:
www.hotels.hu
www.hotelshungary.com
www.budapesthotels.com
www.budapestinfo.hu
www.travelport.hu
www.budapesthotels.hu

On business

The government is tightening economic policy after some frivolity, but foreign investment is still flooding in.

As a small land-locked country without significant natural resources, Hungary is heavily dependent on foreign trade – nearly 50 per cent of GDP is exported. Tourism is a major source of hard currency.

Business hours

The working day is eight hours, usually from 8am to 4pm with a half-hour break for lunch. Industrial workers begin and end the day earlier than office workers. Shops open 10am–6pm, Sat 10am–1pm.

Congresses/fairs

Budapest has a large congress centre, the **Budapest Kongresszusi Központ** (*Jagelló útca 1–3; tel: (06 1) 372 5700; www.bcc.hu*). Information concerning the various trade fairs held during the year may be obtained from the Director of the Budapest Fair Center (HUNGEXPO), X Budapest, Albertirsai útca 10 (postal address: H-1441 Budapest. Pf 44). *Tel: (06 1) 263 6000; www.hungexpo.hu*

Important fairs include International Tourism, Agriculture, Information Technology and Medical Equipment. A major innovation is the Budapest International Wine Festival (usually the second week in September), primarily a showcase for Hungarian wines.

Estate agents (commercial property)

CD Hungary
Vérhalom útca 12–16.
Tel: (06 1) 325 7177.
Cushman & Wakefield Healey & Baker
Deák Palota útca.
Tel: (061) 268 1288.
Jones Lang Lasalle
Alkotás útca 50. Tel: (06 1) 489 0202.

Etiquette

Hungarians are meticulous about greetings: if you meet with a delegation you will be expected to shake hands with each person individually. Business cards are widely used, so take a good supply of your own. Hungarians doing a lot of business with other countries may use the conventional name order, but most will follow the Hungarian order with surname first.

Punctuality is not a Hungarian obsession. If a business partner arrives 15 minutes late, no insult is intended. Business meetings invariably begin with ritual coffee drinking. The decision-making process is slow and the inbred instinct of functionaries to check everything with higher layers of authority is still common.

Money

The exchange rate is fixed daily by the National Bank of Hungary against an average of the US dollar and the euro. The currency is convertible. Rates are posted at exchange kiosks, in banks and at American Express (*Deák Ferenc útca 10, tel: (06 1) 235 4330*). Most banks are open from 8am to 3pm Monday–Thursday and 8am to 1pm on Friday. Exchange kiosks and travel bureaux will change money any time in working hours, and kiosks at weekends.

Services to business people
Accountancy
Hungarian Chamber of Accountants (Magyar Könyvvizsgálói Kamara)
Szinyei Merse útca 8. Tel: (06 1) 473 4500; www.mkvk.hu

Office and secretarial
Regus Kft
The instant office provider, plus video conferencing etc.

Rákóczi útca 42. Tel: (06 1) 267 9111; www.regus.hu

Courier
DHL Magyarország Kft
Kocsis útca 3. Tel: (06 1) 382 3222; fax: (06 1) 204 6666; www.dhl.hu

Dry cleaning
Shirt Express
Home delivery service.
Kámfor útca. Tel: (06 1) 340 8549 or (06 30) 966 5480; www.shirtexpress.hu. Open: Mon–Fri 8am–8pm.

Office supplies
Office Depot
The branch in the Polus Centre shopping mall is open daily.
Tel: (06 1) 414 2341; www.officedepot.hu

Photocopying
Copy General
Lónyay útca 13. Tel: (06 1) 216 8880; www.copygeneral.hu

Translation and interpreting
FORDUNA Fordító és Tolmács Bt
Multilingual services.
Bartók Béla útca 86. Tel: (06 1) 209 2482; www.forduna.hu

Intercontact Budapest Kft
Specialist in bank, legal and technical documents.
Hold útca 15 2/2. Tel: (06 1) 269 1153; www.icontact.hu

Practical guide

Arriving

Visas

Citizens of Australia, New Zealand, the USA, the UK and most countries of continental Europe need only a valid passport and no visa to enter Hungary for a stay of up to 90 days. Everyone else requires a visa, obtainable at Hungarian consulates (usually within 24 hours).

If you are travelling to and fro, get a multiple entry visa for 12 months. Visas are also obtainable at Ferihegy Airport and at main highway border crossings, but not on international trains. Visit *www.mfa.gov.hu* for information.

By air

Ferihegy Airport (*www.bud.hu*) is 24km (15 miles) southwest of the city centre. Terminal 1 is open for low-cost airlines, while other flights use Terminal 2A (*tel: (06 1) 296 7000*) or the adjacent 2B (*tel: (06 1) 296 5052*). Reasonable deals on flights from London to Budapest can be arranged through British Airways and Malév (Hungarian Airlines). From the USA, Malév flies direct. Low-cost airlines like SkyEurope, WizzAir and Germanwings also serve Budapest. The best way of getting into the city is with the airport minibus shuttle, which will deliver you anywhere in the city for a ticket of up to 2,300 Ft. The Airport Minibus desk at the airport is open 5am–1am daily. It can also pick you up

from your accommodation in town to take you to the airport (*tel: (06 1) 296 8555*) 6am–10pm.

Cheaper still is the Reptér-Busz (local bus) which will take you from Terminal 2 via Terminal 1 to the Kőbánya–Kispest metro station and then you can take the metro into town. Reptér-Busz tickets can be bought at the newsagents in the terminal building and also from the bus driver.

Try to avoid taxis standing at the airport: overcharging and unpleasantness are almost inevitable. If you need a taxi, call one by phone (*see p187*).

By rail

Budapest has three international train stations: Nyugati pályaudvar (Western Railway Station), Keleti pályaudvar (Eastern Railway Station) – both in Pest – and Déli pályaudvar (Southern Railway Station) in Buda. Almost all international trains use the Keleti pályaudvar. A timetable can be found on *www.elvira.hu*. There is a direct metro link to the city centre from all three.

The *Thomas Cook European Rail Timetable*, published monthly and providing up-to-date details of most rail and many shipping services throughout Europe, will help you plan a rail journey to, from and around Hungary. You can buy it in the UK from some stations, any office of

Thomas Cook, or by telephoning *(01733) 416477*.

In the USA, visit *www.thomascook.com*

By bus

International bus services arrive at the new Népliget bus terminal (*tel: (06 1) 219 8080; metro: Népliget; tram: 1, 1A; bus: 103 to Népliget*). There are daily buses from Vienna to Budapest run by the Hungarian firm of Volánbusz (*www.volanbusz.hu*) and the Austrian Blaguss line.

Eurolines (*Victoria Coach Station, London, tel: (020) 7730 0202*) and Attila Tours (*36A Kilburn High Road, NW6, tel: (020) 7372 0470*) run a bus service from London in summer.

By car

Border crossings on major roads are open 24 hours (*http://hor.gov.hu*).

By hydrofoil

Hydrofoils run between Vienna and Budapest from April to October. (Information in Vienna from *Handelskai 265*.

Tel: (0043) 1 72 92 161).

In Budapest they dock at the MAHART landing stage of the Belgrád rakpart on the Pest side (*tel: (06 1) 484 4010; www.mahartpassnave.hu*). The journey takes five and a half hours.

The Budapest Card (Budapest Kártya)
This tourist card offers unlimited travel on local public transport, free admission to 60 museums and several sights, free travel on the Children's Railway, a sightseeing tour for half price, reduced-price tickets for cultural and folklore programmes, discounts on thermal baths, as well as in some shops, restaurants, etc.

The card is available at all the main metro ticket offices, tourist information offices, in most hotels and some travel agencies. Price: 6,450 Ft for 48 hours, 7,950 Ft for 72 hours. For information see *www.budapestinfo.hu/en*

Camping
Magyar Camping és Caravanning Club has reductions for Fédération Internationale de Camping et de Caravanning (FIIC) members (*Mária útca 34, tel: (06 1) 267 5255; www.mccc.hu. Open: Mon–Fri 8am–4pm*).

Camp sites
Zugligeti Niche Camping is in the Buda Hills, by the chairlift (*Zugligeti út 101, tel: (06 1) 200 8346; www.campingniche.hu; bus: 158 from Moszkva tér metro*).
Haller Camping (*tel: (06 1) 476 3418; www.hallercamping.hu*) is grassy and central.

Children
Children up to six travel free on public transport. The biggest specialist children's store is **Brendon** at *Váci útca 168*.

Climate

Budapest has a continental climate – very hot in midsummer, bitterly cold in winter (*see chart below for details*).

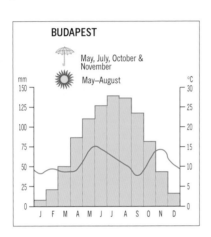

BUDAPEST

May, July, October & November

May–August

WEATHER CONVERSION CHART

25.4mm = 1 inch

$°F = 1.8 × °C + 32$

Conversion tables

See tables on page 181.

Clothes and shoe sizes in Budapest follow those for the rest of Europe.

Crime

Beware of pickpockets, especially in the Váci útca area and at markets, and on crowded public transport vehicles (mainly metros, bus 7 and trams 2, 4 & 6). Do not leave valuables in hotel rooms or cars.

Be careful on trains to and from Hungary, and look after your valuables at Budapest's main stations, especially Keleti. Typical scams include a fellow passenger sitting next to you on a train waiting to depart, putting their large coat next to your belongings; they then move to another seat further down the carriage, swiping your valuables as they go. Alternatively, someone on the platform will ask you a question through the window, while their partner in the carriage steals your things.

Another common crime involves a 'money changer' and two 'undercover policemen'. A tourist will be approached and asked if they want to change some money. If they say no, the money changer will leave, shortly followed by the arrival of two alleged plainclothes police officers. They display false badges or ID, and ask to see all of the tourist's money (to see if any might have come from the money changer). The money will be handled by both men, then replaced in the tourist's wallet which is handed back. However, the 'policemen' will have replaced only the smaller notes, and pocketed the larger ones.

The police emergency number is 107 and the Budapest police headquarters is at Teve útca 4–6, but go first to the nearest police station. The Tourinform office at Süto útca 2 (open daily 8am–8pm) has a special police service for tourists. The Inner City (5th District) Police Department (*Kecskeméti útca 6, tel: (06 1) 317 0711*) also has English-speaking staff.

Customs regulations

Personal effects may be brought in duty-free. Anyone over 16 may bring 200 cigarettes or 50 cigars or 250g of tobacco; also 1 litre of wine and 1 litre of spirits; and small presents up to the value of 175 euros. Pornography and drugs are forbidden, as are firearms without prior authorisation. As Hungary is now an EU member, there is no longer a customs check at the borders with other EU countries.

Money may be taken in and out of the country, but large amounts of cash will arouse suspicions of money laundering. Antiques require an export certificate from the Hungarian National Gallery.

The **Vám és Pénzügyőrség Információs Szogálata** (Customs Information Office) is at *Hungária körút 112–114* (*tel: (06 1) 470 4119; fax: (06 1) 470 4120*), *www.vaminfo.hu* and *http://vam.gov.hu*

Driving
Alcohol
There is absolute prohibition on drinking and driving. Breathalyser tests are common.

Breakdown
The Hungarian Automobile Club (MAK) runs a 'Yellow Angels' (*sárga angyal*) service for motorists in distress, but it can be hard to get through to their emergency number in summer (*188*, 24 hours). The main office is at *Rómer útca* (*tel: (06 1) 345 1800;*

CONVERSION TABLE

FROM	TO	MULTIPLY BY
Inches	Centimetres	2.54
Feet	Metres	0.3048
Yards	Metres	0.9144
Miles	Kilometres	1.6090
Acres	Hectares	0.4047
Gallons	Litres	4.5460
Ounces	Grams	28.35
Pounds	Grams	453.6
Pounds	Kilograms	0.4536
Tons	Tonnes	1.0160

To convert back, for example from centimetres to inches, divide by the number in the third column.

MEN'S SUITS

UK	36	38	40	42	44	46	48
Rest of Europe	46	48	50	52	54	56	58
USA	36	38	40	42	44	46	48

DRESS SIZES

UK	8	10	12	14	16	18
France	36	38	40	42	44	46
Italy	38	40	42	44	46	48
Rest of Europe	34	36	38	40	42	44
USA	6	8	10	12	14	16

MEN'S SHIRTS

UK	14	14.5	15	15.5	16	16.5	17
Rest of Europe	36	37	38	39/40	41	42	43
USA	14	14.5	15	15.5	16	16.5	17

MEN'S SHOES

UK	7	7.5	8.5	9.5	10.5	11
Rest of Europe	41	42	43	44	45	46
USA	8	8.5	9.5	10.5	11.5	12

WOMEN'S SHOES

UK	4.5	5	5.5	6	6.5	7
Rest of Europe	38	38	39	39	40	41
USA	6	6.5	7	7.5	8	8.5

Practical guide

www.autoklub.hu). Reciprocal arrangements cover most European motoring club members.

Documents and insurance

An international driving licence is advisable. Motorists should bring with them the vehicle's registration document and green card insurance. It is obligatory to carry a first-aid kit, a red warning triangle and replacement light bulbs. The vehicle should display a national identification sticker.

Insurance problems and temporary cover are dealt with by **Allianz Hungária Biztosító** (*Bajcsy-Zsilinszky útca 52, tel: (06 1) 301 6111; www.allianz.hu*).

Fuel

Petrol stations (*benzinkút*) sell 98 (extra), 95 (unleaded) and 91 (unleaded) octane petrol and diesel.

Convenient 24-hour petrol stations in Budapest are at Szervita tér 8, Szilágyi Erzsébet fasor 53 (Buda side) and Szentendrei útca 373 (Óbuda).

Parking is difficult in Pest

Parking

In Pest you can forget about street parking. There are a few multistorey or underground car parks in the centre (*Aranykéz útca 4, Szervita tér 8*). Most larger hotels also have a garage.

The capital is sectioned into several parking zones and different parking fees are charged according to the zone – 8am–6pm Mon–Fri and 8am–noon on Saturday. These places are free on Sunday. Parking tickets must be purchased from the nearest ticket machine and displayed behind the windscreen. Minimum parking time is 15 minutes. Traffic police use wheel clamps on illegally parked cars, which may also be towed away. If this happens, contact the nearest police station. Information about parking in Budapest can be found at *www.fkpt.hu*

Traffic regulations

Drive on the right. Yield to traffic from the right unless you are on a priority road (marked with a yellow diamond sign). Seat belts are compulsory front and back (if fitted). Stop for passengers who alight from trams directly into the road (but you may continue if there is a passenger island at the tram stop).

Trams have the right of way, as do buses pulling out from stops. The speed limit in built-up areas is 50kph (31mph), on roads 90kph (56mph) and on motorways 130kph (81mph). It is obligatory to drive with dipped headlights outside the city in daylight hours.

Notify all accidents to the police and report damage to Hungária Biztosító.

Electricity

220 volts 50 cycles AC. Standard continental adaptors are suitable. 100/120 volt appliances require a voltage transformer.

Embassies

Australia *Királyhágó tér 8–9. Tel: (06 1) 457 9777.*

Canada *Ganz útca 12–14. Tel: (06 1) 392 3360.*

New Zealand (Berlin) *Tel: (49)(0)30 206210.*

South Africa *Gárdonyi Géza útca 17. Tel: (06 1) 392 0999.*

UK *Harmincad útca 6. Tel: (06 1) 266 2888.*

USA *Szabadság tér 12. Tel: (06 1) 475 4400.*

Emergencies

General emergency *112*
Ambulance *104*
24-hour emergency medical service (English) *tel: (06 1) 311 1666.*
Chemist (24-hour pharmacies) *Vörösvári útca 86 (Óbuda), Frankel Leó útca 22 (Buda), Alkotás útca 2 (near Déli Railway Station), Béke tér 11, Teréz körút 41 (Pest).*
Dentist
SOS Dental Clinic (24 hours) *Király útca 14. Tel: (06 1) 267 9602.*
Doctor
There are 24-hour casualty

departments at *Hold útca 19 (tel: (06 1) 311 6816)* and *Vihar útca 29 (tel: (06 1) 388 8501).* Private treatment, including 24-hour emergency service from **FirstMed** (*Hattyú útca 14, 5th Floor; tel: (06 1) 224 090. Consultation hours Mon–Thu 8am–7pm, Fri 8am–6pm, Sat 8.30am–1pm*) or **Falck SOS Hungary** (*Kapy útca 49/B; tel: (06 1) 200 0100).*
Fire Brigade *105*
Police *107*
International Emergency *112*

Health

No special vaccinations are needed for Hungary. As in every other part of the world, AIDS is present. Water is safe to drink. Generally visitors must pay for health care, whether state or private. All EU countries have reciprocal arrangements for reclaiming the cost of medical services. UK residents should obtain the European Health Insurance Card from any UK post office.

Many doctors and dentists work privately as well as in the state sector. Lists of those speaking your language may be obtained from your embassy. The underpaid doctors, surgeons and nurses traditionally receive a gratuity from patients, ranging from 20,000 Ft for an operation to at least 1,000 Ft for nurses.

For 24-hour casualty departments see under **Emergencies**. For non-emergency dental treatment go to the Stomatológiai Intézet (Central Dental Institute) of the **Szájsebészeti Klinika** (*Mária útca 52, tel: (06 1) 266 0457).*

Broken bones are dealt with by the **Országos Traumatológiai Kórház** (*Fiumei útca 17, tel: (06 1) 299 7700*).

Holidays

1 January New Year's Day
15 March Anniversary of 1848 revolution
Easter Monday Variable
1 May Labour Day
Whit Monday May/June
20 August St Stephen's and Constitution Day
23 October Anniversary of the 1956 revolution
1 November All Saints' Day
25 and 26 December Christmas

Insurance

Travel insurance is advisable. Check that the policy covers all medical treatment, loss of documents, repatriation, baggage, money and valuables.

Lost property

BKV Talált Tárgyak Osztálya
(Lost Property Office of the Budapest Transport System) is at *Akácfa útca 18* (*tel: (06 1) 267 5299; open Mon–Fri 8am–5pm, to 6pm on Wednesday*).

Otherwise, try the police station nearest to where you lost the item. Passport loss should be reported to your embassy and to the police. Your embassy should be able to advise you what further action needs to be taken.

Maps

Recommended are the *Budapest Atlasz* and *Belváros* (Inner City) map by Cartographia.

Media

Local English-language newspapers are the *Budapest Week* and *The Budapest Sun* and the glossy *Style* magazine. These and foreign publications can be bought at city-centre news-stands and larger hotels. Radio Bridge (102.1 FM) has some English programmes and American news.

Money matters

The Hungarian forint is denominated in 20,000, 10,000, 5,000, 1,000, 500 and 200 Ft notes. Coin denominations are 1, 2, 5, 10, 20, 50 and 100 Ft. The forint is divided into 100 (worthless) fillér.

There are more than 800 ATMs in Budapest giving cash on all common credit and debit cards. Most, but not all, also take Amex, and some take Diners Club cards. Banks are usually open Mon–Thur 8am–3pm, Fri 8am–1pm.

All Hungarian post offices give cash advance on Maestro, Eurocard/MasterCard, Visa and Visa Electron. Look for the *Postamat* sign on a window.

Thomas Cook Traveller's Cheques free you from the hazards of carrying large amounts of cash. Some hotels, shops and restaurants accept them in lieu of cash.

If you need to transfer money, you can use the MoneyGram[SM] Money Transfer service (*tel: 0800 897198*).

Language

PRONUNCIATION

The stress is always on the first syllable.

Vowel sounds

a like the **o** in h**o**t
á like the **u** in h**u**t but twice as long
e as in p**e**n
é as in pl**ay**
i as in s**i**t
í as in m**ea**t
o like the **aw** in p**aw** but shorter
ó the same but longer
ö like the **ur** in f**ur**
ő the same but longer
u as in f**u**ll
ú like the **oo** in s**oo**n
ü as in German f**ü**nf
ű the same but longer

BASIC PHRASES

yes/no	igen/nem
please	kérem (kérek)
you're welcome	szívesen
thank you	köszönöm
(very much)	(szépen)
bon appetit!	egészégére!
hello/goodbye	(informal) szia!
goodbye	viszontlátásra
good morning	jó reggelt
good day	jó napot
good evening	jó estét
goodnight	jó éjszakat
small/large	kicsi, kis/nagy
quickly/slowly	gyorsan/lassan
cold/hot	hideg/meleg
left/right	balra/jobbra
straight ahead	egyenesen előre
where?	hol?
when?	mikor?
why?	miért?
open	nyitva
closed	zárva
how much?	mennyibe kerül?
expensive/cheap	drága/olcsó

Consonants

b, d, f, h, m, n, v, x, z as in English
c like **ts** in ha**ts**
cs like **ch** in **ch**oose
g as in **g**ull
gy like the **d** in **d**uring
j/ly both like **y**
ny like the **n** in **n**ew
r rolled as in Scottish
s like **sh** in **sh**ip
sz like **s** in **s**ea
t as in si**t**
ty like the **tti** in pre**tti**er
zs like the **s** in plea**s**ure.

NUMBERS

1	egy	**6**	hat
2	kettő	**7**	hét
3	három	**8**	nyolc
4	négy	**9**	kilenc
5	őt	**10**	tiz

DAYS OF THE WEEK

Monday	hétfő
Tuesday	kedd
Wednesday	szerda
Thursday	csıtőrtők
Friday	péntek
Saturday	szombat
Sunday	vasárnap

TIME

today	ma
yesterday	tegnap
tomorrow	holnap
day	nap
week	hét
month	hónap
year	év

Opening hours

Food shops are open Mon–Fri 7am or 8am–6pm; Sat 8am–noon or 1pm. Other shops are open Mon–Fri 10am–5pm or 6pm, Sat 9am–1pm (but some do not open on Saturday).

For museums see individual entries; for office hours see **On Business**, *p176*.

Post offices

The main post office (*posta*) and poste restante are at *Városház útca 18* (*tel: (06 1) 485 9041*), *open Mon–Fri 8am–8pm, Sat 8am–2pm*. The post offices at Teréz körút 51 and Baross tér 11C (near Nyugati and Keleti railway stations) have longer opening hours (*www.posta.hu*). The post office in the Tesco hypermarket on Fogarasi útca (*trolleybus 80 to Pillangó útca*) is open 24 hours except holidays.

Public transport

Public transport (*see pp20–21*) is cheap and efficient. All BKV (Budapest Transport Company) tickets and passes except metro-only tickets are valid on all forms of public transport (to the city boundary only on the HÉV). The funicular (*sikló*), chairlift (*libegö*), Danube ships (*hajó*) and ferries (*átkelöhajó*) require separate tickets. Tickets can be purchased at BKV ticket offices, metro stations, newsagents and post offices, and must be validated at station entrances or on the bus, tram, etc, for each stage of the journey. Inspectors can impose spot fines for not doing this.

It is wise to buy a whole-day ticket (*Napijegy*), a three-day one (*Turistajegy & Napra*), or a weekly pass (*Hetijegy*), valid on all forms of transport. You need to write your name on the weekly pass, and show photo ID if requested.

Hungarian and EU citizens over the age of 65 may travel free of charge on all public transport except the funicular, chairlift and Danube ships. Photo ID is required.

Public transport runs between 4 or 5am and around 11pm, but night buses with 900 numbers (like 956, etc) operate between 11pm and 4am daily. HÉV suburban trains are useful for visiting Szentendre (*see pp128–30*) and Ráckeve (*see pp134–6*).

Scheduled boats (*vonali hajójárat*) on the Danube run in both directions between Boráros tér and Csillaghegy (*Piroska útca*) daily, May–August. Tickets are sold on board. For timetables see *www.bkv.hu/eygeb/hajo.html*

The *Centre of Budapest* map and the *Transport Network* map (Budapest Közlekedési Háhózata), published by the BKV and sold at the ticket offices and sometimes by the Budapest Tourist Board, are very useful. Timetables are posted at the stops and can also be obtained from *www.bkv.hu*. The black number is for the 'slow' line, the red for the 'fast' line with fewer stops and, sometimes, a different route.

Sustainable tourism

Thomas Cook is a strong advocate of ethical and fairly traded tourism and believes that the travel experience should be as good for the places visited as it is for the people who visit them. That's why we firmly support The Travel Foundation: a charity that develops solutions to help improve and protect holiday destinations, their environment, traditions and culture. To find out what you can do to make a positive difference to the places you travel to and the people who live there, please visit *www.thetravelfoundation.org.uk*

Taxis

The most reliable are: **Fötaxi** (*tel: (06 1) 222 2222 or toll-free 0680 222 222*), **Buda Taxi** (*tel: (06 1) 233 3333*), and **City Taxi** (*tel: (01) 211 1111*).

Budapest metro & rail network

Practical guide

Telephones

The area code for Budapest city is 1 (not to be used from within the city, and calls from the UK *only* use 01); and 36 for calls inside the country; from elsewhere in Hungary to Budapest dial 06 1 before the local 7-digit numbers. For calls between towns in Hungary dial 06, then the town area code, then the local number. Dial *198* for domestic enquiries (or see *www.tudakozo.t-com.hu*) and *199* for international enquiries. Mobile servers begin with 20, 30 or 70.

For calls abroad, first dial 00. The international operator is 09. Country codes: **Australia** *61*, **Ireland** *353*, **New Zealand** *64*, **UK** *44*, **USA** and **Canada** *1*.

Time

Hungary is one hour ahead of GMT (Greenwich Mean Time), six hours ahead of EST (Eastern Standard Time), and nine ahead of PST (Pacific Standard Time). Add one hour for summer time (April to September).

Tipping

Porters, maids, cloakroom attendants, guides, garage attendants, waiters and gypsy violinists will all expect tips of between 100 and 500 Ft (10 to 15 per cent for waiters and taxi drivers).

Toilets

There are plenty of public toilets in Budapest. Leave a few forints in the saucer by the door. Signs – *mosdó* (WC); *férfi* (men); *női* (women).

Tourist information

Everything you want to know about travel and events in Budapest and Hungary can be answered by **Tourinform** (*Sütő útca 2, open daily 8am–8pm*). Also see *www.hungary.com* or *www.tourinform.hu*. Tourinform call centre (24 hours): *(06 1) 438 8080*. Tourinform hotline (24 hours) from abroad: *+ 36 30 30 30600*; from Hungary (freephone): *06 80 630 800*.

The **Budapest Tourist Board** (*tel: 06 1) 266 7477; www.budapestinfo.hu/en* also has information offices at: *Liszt Ferenc tér 11, tel: (06 1) 322 4098; Szentháromsdg tér (Castle District), tel: (06 1) 488 0475; Western Railway Station, platform 10, tel: (06 1) 302 8580; M1 and M7 motorways by the AGIP complex; Ferihegy Airport in Terminals 2A and 2B, tel: (06 1) 438 8080.*

Travellers with disabilities

Facilities for travellers with disabilities are generally poor. Information is available from the Hungarian Disabled Association (MEOSZ) (*San Marco útca 76, tel: (06 1) 388 5529; www.meosz.hu; open: Mon–Fri 8am–4pm*).

Budapest's Central Market

Index

Acknowledgements

Thomas Cook Publishing wishes to thank the following photographers, libraries and associations for their assistance in the preparation of this book, and to whom the copyright belongs.

TOURISM OFFICE OF BUDAPEST 50, 148, 149
MICHAEL TRAFFORD 157
PICTURES COLOUR LIBRARY 20, 74, 147
WENDY WRANGHAM 13, 19, 25, 33, 41, 56, 72, 79, 89, 156, 169, 182, 188
WIKIMEDIA COMMONS 85, 103 (Csörföly D), 119 (Gabor Eszes), 135 (Csanády)
WORLD PICTURES/PHOTOSHOT 1, 10, 17, 84, 101, 123, 128

The remaining pictures are held in the AA PHOTO LIBRARY and were taken by: KEN PATTERSON, with the exception of pages 21, 26, 29, which were taken by ERIC MEACHER, and pages 27, 87, 174, taken by PETER WILSON.

Index: MARIE LORIMER

For CAMBRIDGE PUBLISHING MANAGEMENT LIMITED:
Project editor: KAREN BEAULAH
Typesetter: TREVOR DOUBLE
Proofreader: IAN FAULKNER

SEND YOUR THOUGHTS TO
BOOKS@THOMASCOOK.COM

We're committed to providing the very best up-to-date information in our travel guides and constantly strive to make them as useful as they can be. You can help us to improve future editions by letting us have your feedback. If you've made a wonderful discovery on your travels that we don't already feature, if you'd like to inform us about recent changes to anything that we do include, or if you simply want to let us know your thoughts about this guidebook and how we can make it even better – we'd love to hear from you.

Send us ideas, discoveries and recommendations today and then look out for your valuable input in the next edition of this title.

Emails to the above address, or letters to Travellers Series Editor, Thomas Cook Publishing, PO Box 227, Coningsby Road, Peterborough PE3 8SB, UK.

Please don't forget to let us know which title your feedback refers to!